SO YOU WANT TO BE A SUPERVISOR!

SO YOU WANT TO BE A SUPERVISOR!

Elton T. Reeves

American Management Association, Inc.

International standard book number: 0-8144-5244-2
Library of Congress catalog card number: 70-141678

Fourth printing

For Delores and Rosemary
with love from Daddy

Foreword

THERE are many thousands of employees who want to become members of management. This book is intended to provide a developmental plan which will help them achieve this goal.

Elton T. Reeves

Contents

What It's Like
to Be a Supervisor

W HEN an employee starts his climb up the management ladder, his first step will be his biggest: from subordinate to supervisor. Of course, he will still be somebody's subordinate—but he will also be a *manager*. The qualitative differences between his former rank-and-file status and his new managerial status will be tremendous. They go beyond a new list of job duties. They involve differences in perspective, in basic concepts, in emphasis, in the sources of job satisfaction, in status, in relationships with other people in the organization.

Recognizing and accepting these differences is a major requirement of preparing to be a supervisor. It is just as important an element to consider when you are deciding whether or not you really *want* to be a supervisor. No chapter in a book can adequately convey the full impact of how your whole life will change with the transition from subordinate to supervisor. But this book can give you enough of a picture to enable you to draw up a balance sheet of pluses and minuses. On one side of the balance sheet would be what you consider the advantages of being a supervisor. On the other side would be the disadvantages. The moment of truth arrives, of course, when you must weigh one side against the other. To come up with a sound decision, you will need all the objectivity at your command, in evaluating both yourself and the job factors involved.

Why Some Supervisors Have Split Personalities

The overriding difference between supervision and nonsupervision is an obvious one—but at the same time it often poses the greatest difficulty for a new supervisor. Put simply, this difference can be characterized as *managing versus doing.* And the conflict that this difference frequently creates might be called supervisory split personality. This paralyzing disorder results from a tug of war between the new role of leader and administrator and the old role of skilled, conscientious worker. The supervisor's new job requires him to be the first, but he may still see himself as the second.

Supervisors trapped in this conflict have not accepted their changed role. Perhaps you yourself have seen one of these examples:

• The office manager who rechecks and recalculates every clerical procedure himself.

- The shop foreman who spends most of his time on production records and machine maintenance.
- The stockroom head who keeps tinkering with his new parts filing system, while neglecting the problems of motivating his subordinates.

The more highly skilled a new supervisor is technically, the greater his difficulty may be in adjusting to the fact that he should now be a manager, not a doer. His conscience nags him either way: He knows he must delegate tasks, yet he is not sure his subordinates will do the job as thoroughly and accurately as he would himself.

Despite initial difficulties, most new supervisors eventually make a successful transition to their new role. Some do not, and this raises doubts as to whether they considered this key factor seriously enough before becoming supervisors. As you yourself are evaluating this factor on your balance sheet, keep in mind this basic definition of management: *getting things done through other people.*

This concept, of course, leads to other substantial differences between your present role and your future role as a supervisor. One is in the amount and quality of responsibility that you will have. Now you are responsible only for performing your own job satisfactorily. Your task is to meet *your* quota, maintain the quality of *your* work, keep *your* costs down, watch out for *your* safety, maintain *your* attendance record, meet *your* deadlines. If you mentally expand your responsibility for these factors to cover every employee in your department, you can easily see how radically changed the depth and breadth of your responsibility as a supervisor will be.

To help you fulfill your new responsibility, your authority will expand correspondingly. As a rank-and-file employee, you are directed in your work. As a supervisor, you will still be directed—although far less closely—but you will suddenly find yourself with the authority to assign jobs, to give orders and directions, to hand out disciplinary penalties, to purchase equipment.

In other words, you will have the authority to make important decisions. You may be employing your decision-making skills on your present job, but the range of your decisions is narrowly restricted. Your supervisory decision-making power will be much broader—and your decisions will probably be more difficult and complex. Often they must be made on the spot and under pressure; yet seldom will you have all the facts you want before you must make up your mind.

Nevertheless, decision making *can* be one of a supervisor's most rewarding activities. There is nothing more gratifying than to make a tough decision and see it justified by the results. A question you must ask yourself, however, is whether you are willing to make firm decisions even when all the facts are not in and you run the risk of error.

As a supervisor, you will have two kinds of authority: One might be called *external* authority—this is the power bestowed upon you by your organization. But in addition to this, you should have *internal* authority. Obviously, no two supervisors wield exactly the same authority in the same positions, even though their job descriptions give them exactly the same amount. Internal authority makes the difference. This is the authority the supervisor commands by earning the respect of his subordinates. In many ways, it is the more important kind of authority, because it brings forth the kind of cooperation and enthusiasm that makes for a top-performing department.

What other changes will you find as a new supervisor? You will, of course, have more status, which will lead to broadened social contacts with people in the organization you had no opportunity to know before, such as other supervisors and members of higher management. On the other side of the coin, however, is the fact that although you may make some new friendships you may have to sacrifice some old ones. Without the ties of similar jobs and status, your friendships with former fellow workers may fade.

Back on the plus side, your new status will make you privy to inside information about your organization that you would be unlikely to receive now. You will know more about what is going on and more of the thinking behind top-management decisions. This, of course, will be useful in helping you learn how your organization functions at higher levels. In addition, receiving confidential information is a mark of status that you may find an attractive feature of a managerial job.

Better compensation—both in pay and fringe benefits —is an important plus for supervisory jobs. As a general rule, a supervisor makes at least 25 percent more than the highest-paid employee reporting to him. There are exceptions. For example, it is possible for an employee to make more than his supervisor for short periods of heavy overtime. But there is no doubt that, overall, a supervisor has a far brighter economic future than does a rank-and-file employee.

Although the supervisor's health benefits are about the same as those of his subordinates, his vacation and sick-leave privileges are usually more liberal. Depending on his level, he may also receive bonuses.

Again, however, there is another side to the coin. Although a supervisor has greater opportunities for higher income, he sacrifices the job security he enjoyed as a rank-and-file employee. The chances are good that you now have some kind of job protection based on your length of service with your organization. If you belong to a union, formal seniority protects you from whimsical or unfair discharge. If business slumps, you know that you will not be laid off while an employee with less seniority remains.

As a supervisor, you will have far less formal protection. The possibility always exists that you can be dismissed for a serious error in judgment. We are not saying that your superiors would do such a thing, but there is no union contract to stop them from it. Your security could also be in danger when there is a profit squeeze on your company. By increasing the span of control—that is, the number of subordinates reporting to each supervisor—a company can get along with fewer supervisors.

These possibilities are not mentioned to alarm you or discourage you from aspiring to a supervisory job. They are included so that you can draw up an accurate balance sheet that will reflect the drawbacks as well as the benefits of being a manager. You could not come to a sound decision if you ignored them.

Nor can you ignore another major change that inevitably accompanies a promotion to managerial ranks: the loss of leisure time. At the start particularly, there is so much to learn and so much to do that you may have to neglect your family, your hobbies, and your sports interests. And though this condition may ease a bit when you become better versed in your job, it will be a way of life as long as you are a manager. Unlike the nonsupervisory employee, you may have to work extra hours without payment for overtime. In addition, you may often find yourself taking your job home with you, to read reports or brood about a tough decision you must make. Naturally, this factor of supervisory life will go on the debit side of your balance sheet. The question you must eventually answer is whether it is too high a price to pay for what is on the plus side.

How do you react to competition? That is another inevitable part of supervisory life. Once you have taken that giant step into the first level of management, the chances are that you will soon set your goals higher. If you visualize your organization's management structure as a pyramid, with supervisors forming the base and the chief executive at the top, you can easily see why the climb gets tougher at each successive level. As an ambitious supervisor, you will be competing for your next promotion with other equally ambitious supervisors. This doesn't rule out friendly relationships with your colleagues, but it does mean that, friendly or not, they are competing with you for advancement. You are no longer protected by seniority and a negotiated line of progression. You are strictly on your own, and whether you welcome competition or feel threatened by it should figure importantly in your thinking about management as a career.

Competition is but one form of pressure you will discover when you become a supervisor. There are other pressures that you probably do not face in your present job. They will come at you from below, from above, and from all sides. You can expect demands and grievances from your subordinates which may conflict with equally urgent demands from higher management. It is small wonder that a supervisor often feels that he is a battlefield for opposing forces—the "man in the middle." No matter what he does, he knows that it will be impossible to completely satisfy both his people and his management.

Added to that are lateral pressures from fellow supervisors. You must cooperate with them in order to get your job done, but sometimes it will seem to you that you are doing all the cooperating while they are making all the demands on you so that they can achieve their own objectives.

All these pressures can cause stress. The supervisor, unlike the rank-and-file employee, is faced with problems that are often complex and ambiguous rather than simple and clear-cut. Ambiguity confronts the supervisor, for example, in situations where there is no one correct answer to the problem at hand that will satisfy everyone concerned and be consistent with his own values. But he must make decisions, and in doing so he is constantly forced to compromise.

There is simply no way to eliminate stress completely from a supervisory job. In fact, some stress is not necessarily bad; there is considerable evidence that mild stress stimulates performance. Nevertheless, some people prefer to minimize the stress in their lives. Therefore, anyone considering a managerial career should recognize and accept the fact that it will mean an increase in stress.

What we have been saying about the demands of a supervisory job can perhaps best be summed up in the word *commitment*. Being a supervisor means that you must commit more of yourself to your job than you probably do in your present position. Such a commitment necessarily interferes with your personal and family activities and often taxes your psychological and physical resources.

Drawing Up a Balance Sheet

We have now described briefly the major features of the typical supervisory job. Not all such jobs are exactly alike, of course, and specific factors may play a larger role in some than in others. By and large, however, you can expect to find all these elements to some degree in any supervisory job.

Although we can tell you about the features of supervision, what we cannot tell you is what they mean to you specifically. This is something that you yourself must decide with the help of only some general guidelines from us. The reason is simple: You know yourself best.

The immediate task ahead of you is not to evaluate your *ability* to be a successful supervisor. It is, rather, to evaluate your *desire* to be one—to determine whether you are ready to make the necessary commitment to achieve this goal. Now is the time to make a firm decision one way or the other. Unless you can give a strong affirmative answer, you would be unwise to invest valuable time in an ambitious self-development program. And your underlying lack of commitment would inevitably affect the quality of your performance if you *were* promoted to supervisor.

All of this calls for introspection on your part—looking within yourself. True introspection demands a degree of objectivity (no one can be completely objective about himself) that you may not be used to exercising. Most people look into their mental mirrors with astigmatic vision. Too often they see a distorted image of themselves rather than what they really are. This can lead to major problems when you are attempting to make what is truly a momentous decision.

In analyzing yourself, one of the most essential questions you must ask is what you want out of life and whether a supervisory job can help you attain your goals. Be as specific as possible in your answers. Vague phrases like "happiness in life" will certainly not help you to decide for or against a managerial career. Try to pinpoint more precisely what happiness means to you. Does it mean freedom from stress? Or does it mean the excitement and challenge of solving difficult problems? Does it mean tinkering with machines? Or does it mean working with people, helping them to grow and develop in their jobs? Does it mean having power and authority? Or does it mean being responsible to no one but yourself?

Such self-analysis is not a simple process. What we want out of life is often not clear even to ourselves. The result is conflicting desires that make it difficult to come to a firm decision about choosing a career. The best we can do, in many cases, is assign specific factors to the plus or minus side of the balance sheet and then weigh their importance.

The chances are that you will assign such factors as better compensation and more status to the plus side of your balance sheet. Other factors, such as less leisure time and less job protection would almost always go on the minus side. But where you place most of the factors depends on the results of your introspection, because the choices are far more subjective. You may relish the idea of having more responsibility, or you may prefer to be free of it. You may want broader decision-making power, or you may want your decisions made for you. You may dislike pressure, or you may thrive on it.

It is essential that you be honest with yourself. If you

have already been seriously considering a management career, have you been deluding yourself into thinking that you can enjoy the greater pay and status of being a supervisor while at the same time avoid the added responsibility and pressure that are established features of the position? If so, perhaps responsibility and pressure should be listed on the minus side of the balance sheet.

Once you have assigned each major feature of a supervisory job to the appropriate column, you come to what is an even more difficult task: weighing each feature's relative importance. Again, we say, be honest, because your entire future is at stake. Is it of major or minor importance to you that as a supervisor you would have less time to spend with your family or on your leisure-time activities? Is this disadvantage offset by the additional income that would provide a higher standard of living for you and your family? How important is it to you that you might have to give up some close friendships with your fellow workers?

The answers to these specific questions will lead to the final question you must ask yourself: Am I willing to pay the price? No matter what your goal, its achievement must be paid for. Every success implies a certain amount of failure. The dedication and commitment that real success in any field requires means that some other areas of life must be short-changed.

Figure 1 is a balance sheet form listing all the features of a supervisory job that we have discussed. Take your time in sorting out and weighing the various factors you must consider. Add any other factors you think should play a part in your decision. When you have decided that a factor should go into the plus or minus column, indicate its

Figure 1. Balance sheet

Do I Want to Be a Supervisor?

Factor	Rating					
	Plus			Minus		
1. More managing, less doing	1	2	3	1	2	3
2. More responsibility	1	2	3	1	2	3
3. More authority	1	2	3	1	2	3
4. Broader decision making	1	2	3	1	2	3
5. More status	1	2	3	1	2	3
6. Changed relationships with fellow workers	1	2	3	1	2	3
7. More inside information	1	2	3	1	2	3
8. Better compensation	1	2	3	1	2	3
9. Less job security	1	2	3	1	2	3
10. Less leisure time	1	2	3	1	2	3
11. More competition	1	2	3	1	2	3
12. Greater pressures	1	2	3	1	2	3
13. Greater commitment	1	2	3	1	2	3
Total	+			−		

relative weight by circling 1, 2, or 3 in ascending order of importance. Adding up the totals should give you a fairly reliable idea of which way the balance sheet leans.

You will then be ready for that moment of truth—your decision on whether or not you want to be a supervisor. If it is *no,* then you will stick to your present job, satisfied that the grass is not greener in the next pasture. If it is *yes,* you are ready to start considering the specific skills and abilities required for successful supervision. We will discuss those elements in the next chapter.

2

Skills and Abilities You Will Need

As you read this chapter, you may not yet have made your final decision on whether to try for a supervisory position. This would be perfectly reasonable, because although Chapter 1 told you about some important features of the supervisor's job, it did not tell you what specific skills and abilities you would need to be successful at that job. It would be unrealistic for you to try for promotion *only* because you like the idea of being a supervisor, but without knowing what it takes to be successful.

No two successful supervisors are exactly alike in the way they operate. Suppose you had the opportunity to watch ten different first-rate supervisors on a typical day—

that is, if a supervisor ever has a typical day. You would see that although they might all be equally effective, each puts the stamp of his own individuality on his methods of achieving his goals.

But despite the wide variety of unique touches a supervisor may apply to his managerial methods, you will find certain basic skills and abilities that each has in common with other top-performing supervisors. Attaining these skills and abilities will be the prime goal of your self-development program. It is possible that you may already have some of these skills and abilities to a certain extent; in fact, you may be using them on your present job. Others may be completely unfamiliar to you. If you possess the basic capacity for supervising, however, these skills and abilities can be strengthened through a carefully planned and executed self-development program.

The rest of this chapter describes a dozen of the most important supervisory skills and abilities.

1. Functional Ability

What do we mean by functional ability? Broadly, it may be defined as the ability to function effectively under any circumstances the supervisor has to face in his job. Obviously, functional ability is not a specific technical skill. It is made up partly of attitude, partly of experience, partly of intelligence, and partly of skills such as communicating and decision making. One way to measure functional ability is by how well a supervisor applies his skills, intelligence, and experience to solving any problem that confronts him.

Functional ability is tremendously important to a supervisor because, as emphasized in Chapter 1, he faces a continual barrage of new problems and pressures. As long as deadlines are lenient and decisions easy, he may get by. But when schedules get. tight, work piles up, employees are unexpectedly absent, supplies don't arrive on time, conflicting demands come in from all sides—it is then that the supervisor must demonstrate his functional ability. Unless he can cope with these problems, and not collapse under them, he can never expect to be a successful manager.

This means he must learn to function under conditions of extreme stress, somewhat like an astronaut who must learn to function during critical emergencies in outer space. It means he must also be able to function when he feels frustrated in getting what he wants. It means he must accept the inevitability of obstacles and roadblocks and try to break through them or work around them. He must recognize that things will go wrong and that he must be able to concentrate on making them right rather than bemoaning his fate. He must be willing to seek alternatives when he cannot get exactly what he wants.

2. Planning

Planning is a fundamental supervisory skill with which you may not be too familiar in your present job. You may have had small need to do much planning of your work, at least for more than a few days at a time. As a supervisor, however, you must think much farther ahead and you have many more elements to juggle in your planning. Without

15

plans, future events are left to chance, and Lady Luck is notoriously fickle. The more fully a supervisor plans the work of his department, the less likely he is to find himself fighting unexpected crises and emergencies, and the more likely he is to achieve the goals that he has set for his department.

That means a supervisor must spend much of his time in planning for the future. What is happening today should be a result of the plans he made a week or a month or a year ago, and it should help him plan for goals a week or a month or a year *ahead.*

It is essential, then, for a potential supervisor to develop his skill in planning if he is to run a productive, goal-achieving department. Indeed, planning skills are necessary for the very foundation of the department's whole effort. Careful planning transforms the department's purpose into action by setting up concrete objectives. And it gives the supervisor greater control over the direction and progress of his department's activities.

If the planning you do on your job is relatively simple, you may wonder why it should be considered so important a skill in supervision. The answer is that supervisory planning takes a tremendous jump in complexity over planning that you might be doing now. In your present position, your planning might consist in deciding how you are going to complete two or three assignments over a period of a few days. As a supervisor, however, you may have half a dozen different goals to be met by your department, and in order to achieve these goals you must juggle a number of elements, such as men, materials, equipment, and money. Faced with this kind of complexity, you will find that planning is indeed an important and a difficult skill. Later in the book, you will find some useful suggestions for improving your planning skills through study and actual practice.

3. Organizing

You may have even less experience in organizing than in planning. Since you are responsible for only your own job, you need not concern yourself with coordinating the rest of the jobs in your department. As a supervisor, however, your skill at organizing your team will be a key factor to your success or failure. The smooth functioning of any group activity depends on efficient organization.

What is skill in organizing? Basically, it may be defined as *how well a supervisor coordinates all the resources of his department—men, money, materials, equipment, and methods—to reach the goals of his department.* To put it another way, skillful organizing means having the right man on the right job at the right time with the right material and equipment.

This is not so difficult, of course, if you have only one job to consider. Again, as with planning, the supervisor is faced with a far more complex challenge. It is no easy task to coordinate perhaps 20 different jobs so they function efficiently together rather than pull in 20 different directions.

What are the elements of organizing skill? Among them are:

• The ability to establish clear-cut duties and objectives for every job under the supervisor's control.

• The ability to assign clearly defined authority and accountability to each job.

• The ability to coordinate jobs through clear-cut channels of communication.

- The ability to schedule department work efficiently.
- The ability to develop organizational methods that will accomplish specific department goals.

4. Controlling

When we use the word controlling to describe this important supervisory skill, we are not referring to, as you might assume, controlling subordinates. Actually, the idea of continuous, eagle-eyed surveillance of employees is directly contrary to progressive management concepts because it stifles employee initiative and responsibility. Controlling, to a supervisor, should mean controlling results—making sure that results conform to the supervisor's plan and that his department is making good headway toward the goals he has set for it. This includes, of course, making sure that employee performance is measuring up to standards.

Controlling, though it might be part of your present job, becomes immensely more complicated on a managerial level. Currently, you are responsible for the results of your own performance, and the goals of your job are limited in number. But put yourself in the mental shoes of a supervisor who is responsible for the performance of 20 different jobs and has probably set a number of different goals for his department. This gives him a lot to keep track of. For his department and for each of the jobs in his department, he must keep tabs on such factors as production, quality, cost, waste, maintenance, and efficiency. If he fails to do this skillfully, he may wake up one day to find that none of his department's goals are being achieved, and it is too late to do anything about it now.

Controlling is one of the more technical supervisory skills, but anyone with a reasonably well-organized mind can become proficient at it. Moreover, there are a number of useful tools available to the supervisor that make it easier for him to learn at the earliest possible moment when department plans are going off target. Such tools might be charts, graphs, tables, or other kinds of systematic presentation.

In addition, the computer will play an increasingly important role in helping a supervisor control results in his department. In another chapter, we will discuss the supervisor's relationship with the computer and how he can familiarize himself with the role it might play in his job.

A tool, of course, is only as good as the skill with which it is used. Many supervisors who lack skill in the controlling function tend to have an unnecessarily elaborate system of reports and controls that get them too bogged down in meaningless information to see what is really important. One of the fundamental skills in controlling is the ability of the supervisor to wisely select the things he should know and be willing to do without the things he really does not need to know.

5. Oral Communication

If you think back to our basic definition of management—getting things done through other people—it is easy to see why skill in communication is so important an asset to a supervisor. Since effective communication is his basic tool for managing, he will find that he spends most of his day involved in some form of this process.

In fact, the supervisor is at the center of his organization's communications network. He must communicate upward, to let higher management know what is going on, so it will have the facts on which to base intelligent decisions. He must communicate laterally to his fellow supervisors, to facilitate coordination and teamwork. He must communicate downward to his subordinates, so that he can be effective in giving orders, training, delegating, disciplining, handling grievances, motivating, and every other area of supervision.

As a supervisor, most of your communicating will be oral: making and receiving phone calls, giving and receiving instructions, leading and participating in meetings, counseling and training subordinates, getting the facts on department problems, negotiating with the union steward and with other managers, and more. To give you an idea of how much of your time you will spend communicating orally, one manager who was observed over a 35-day period was discovered in only 12 instances to have spent 15 minutes *without* talking. A study in another company found that managers spend, on the average, 80 percent of their time talking.

Despite this, potential supervisors often focus little attention and effort on developing their skill in oral communication. They simply do not think of it as a skill that must be improved, but rather as something that comes naturally and that they already know how to do effectively. In actuality, however, communicating is a complex process that requires great skill, and it is skill that must be learned. This is not to say that you may not already be an effective communicator. But as a supervisor, you will be faced with new and challenging demands on your abilities in this area. You will be communicating with far more people than in your present job, and each person will be different. Your communicating will probably deal with more complex matters, often requiring a certain amount of subtlety. Much of the time, your communicating will be intended to get people to do something, and such communication calls for careful planning and executing.

Moreover, psychological barriers can frequently impede clear communication, and a supervisor should know what these barriers are and how to surmount them. Words mean different things to different people, our prejudices influence what we hear, our emotional state of mind can also color what we hear, and so on. A supervisor must be aware of all these factors that influence communication if he is to communicate effectively and persuasively.

Listening, as well as talking, is an important part of oral communication. The potential supervisor may tend to ignore this aspect of communication, however, because most of us prefer talking to listening. As one author put it, "Bores are people who talk when you wish them to listen." Moreover, effective listening requires work and concentration—it is not just a matter of opening your ears. When planning your self-development program, therefore, you will be wise to allot time to improving this important skill.

6. Written Communication

Your present job may already involve a substantial amount of written communication in the form of letters, memos, and reports. However, many rank-and-file jobs, particularly in industry, require almost no written communication. If this is true of your present job, you can expect a quantum jump in the amount of written communication your new job demands. Even production supervisors must deal with what may seem like a huge amount of paper work. Paper work may not be your favorite activity when you become a supervisor, but it is a necessary one, and you would be delinquent in an important supervisory skill if you failed to learn how to communicate effectively in writing. Regardless of whether you have had much or little experience, you can undoubtedly improve your writing skills. Good technique in writing reports and memos will serve you well because such written communication may be seen and appreciated by higher levels of management than you could ever reach orally. Thus the ability to write a clear, concise report can be an important factor in your eventual promotion to better management jobs.

Often, too, a written report can be more effective than an oral one. Suppose, for instance, that you have discussed a project orally with your boss and failed to make your point. If he said no to the project because he did not fully understand it, a carefully constructed report might well change his mind. Or if the person you want to communicate with is quick to cross swords in a conversation, or if the written word impresses him more than the spoken one, your best bet would be a written report.

Regardless of your present level of competence at writing, you can do much to strengthen this vital skill, and we will suggest some sources of help later on.

7. Company Orientation

What do we mean by company orientation? The term does not quite fit into the same class as the first six factors we have discussed; these are skills and abilities, whereas company orientation is basically an attitude. In Chapter 1, we mentioned that taking a managerial job entailed a major commitment on your part. Part of this commitment consists of developing a wider perspective than you may have as a rank-and-file employee. Currently, you are responsible for only your own job. If you perform it competently you have discharged your obligations. Once you are promoted to supervisor, however, you have moved into the ranks of those with decision-making power who are actually guiding the destinies of the company. You could scarcely fulfill this responsibility unless you were able to relate well to company objectives and programs. Indeed, no man or woman should even go into management unless he or she has a genuine concern for the goals of his company and his own role in helping to achieve them.

Often, the "managerial attitude" is interpreted too narrowly to mean that the supervisor should automatically agree with everything that he is told by his superiors. This concept actually represents the opposite of a healthy managerial attitude, because it ultimately shortchanges the company. For example, if higher management is developing plans for a new method or system, it would hurt the company if a supervisor saw serious flaws in the plans but remained silent out of "loyalty."

As one president of a large company put it recently, "If a supervisor feels that one of his subordinates has been unfairly treated and raises what he considers a legitimate grievance; if he is less than enthusiastic about accepting a situation that seems to him unreasonable; if he questions the wisdom of a course of action that has been prescribed by higher management—he is not being disloyal to his company. He is acting in good faith and he is a more valuable member of the company than the supervisor who will go along, like a chameleon, with almost any change or decision because it seems to be expedient at the moment to do so."

Higher management, of course, does not want supervisors who deliberately disobey its orders and policies. It wants a loyalty that is based on common sense, experienced judgment, a sense of fairness, and a respect for the company's interests. Thus the supervisor can respect and carry out company rules and the orders of his superiors, and yet offer his superiors constructive disagreement when he feels it is justified. He can contribute his ideas for improvement, both in his department and the whole company, by communicating a need, proposal, or disagreement through proper organizational channels. He can keep his superiors informed of the things they should know—both good and bad—about his department. He can cooperate with other supervisors and consider how his actions will affect their operations. He can speak well of the company in his contacts with customers, suppliers, and other outside people. He can keep company goals in mind, rather than think only in terms of his own department.

This, then, is company orientation translated into action. As a potential supervisor, you can do much to achieve this management attitude in your self-development program. Later on in the book, we suggest several do-it-yourself projects that can help you develop the broader horizons you need in order to contribute to both your own success and the success of your company.

8. Leadership

It may seem strange to you that we are including leadership in the list of desirable supervisory skills and abilities. It is, of course, a desirable quality, but you may not think of it as a skill or ability that can be developed. There is a common misconception about leadership: that you are either born with this quality or you are not. It may be true that some people have a natural affinity for leadership. But it is equally true that leadership potential must be developed into finished skills; therefore, a supervisor who has worked hard and intelligently to make the most of his leadership potential may be a far more effective leader than one who may have been born with more natural leadership qualities but has failed to develop them. Thus it is not strictly true to say that "leaders are born, not made." Leaders *are* made—by the opportunities they find to develop the leadership talents that are latent within them.

Before trying to develop his leadership skills, the potential supervisor should be clear in his mind just what leadership is and what it is not. It is not, as he may think, the same as authority. A title on the office door does not make you a leader any more than a baseball uniform makes you a major-league baseball player. This can easily be seen in a department whose supervisor is an ineffectual leader. The chances are that one of his subordinates—despite having no official authority—has moved into the leadership vacuum in the department by virtue of his personal qualities. What we are saying, then, is that leadership consists of an inner authority, not one that is conferred by the organization. In trying to get things done through others, the

25

genuine leader does not depend on threats and coercion, but on his own competence, personality, and methods of motivating and directing.

This means, naturally, that the supervisor must show leadership in many different areas of his job, and each area requires specific skills. But there are certain basic leadership principles that will be unchanging no matter what the specific situation or problem may be. Here are some of them:

The leader initiates action.
The leader maintains discipline.
The leader sets an example.
The leader motivates his subordinates.
The leader builds morale.
The leader backs up his people.
The leader delegates responsibility.
The leader inspires confidence.
The leader stands up under stress.
The leader has a wide range of skills.
The leader is decisive.
The leader solves problems.
The leader communicates effectively.
The leader develops his subordinates.

Looking over this list should convince you that leadership skills can be developed. You cannot successfully delegate, solve problems, make sound decisions, motivate your subordinates, or communicate by intuition alone. There are many ways in which you can work on developing your leadership skills even before you become a supervisor. Since leadership is largely concerned with how you relate to your subordinates, you can develop your skills by learning more about people and their behavior, both as individuals and in groups. You can also put yourself into situations that give you an opportunity to actually practice leadership skills even though you are not yet a supervisor.

This study and practice will give you the basic groundwork from which you can then go on to set your own leadership style. Always keep in mind that there is no rigidly right or wrong way to be a leader. You should not feel that you must force yourself into a role that makes you feel awkward and uncomfortable. Subordinates can quickly spot "formula" leadership and they are quick to resent it because they feel they are being manipulated for your own purposes. There is no formula when it comes to practicing leadership. Instead, your success as a leader calls for the blending of your own personal capacities with sound leadership principles, applied flexibly but consistently.

9. Decision Making

Decisions, decisions, decisions—the supervisor's day is full of them. His skill in solving problems with sound decisions is essential to his success as a manager. He must know how to consider alternative courses of action, predict the probable results of each, and decide which is the right one to take. Once he has made a decision, he must be able to live with it and not agonize endlessly over whether he did the right thing.

In thinking about the decision-making aspect of your supervisory job, you may visualize yourself as the stereotyped whirlwind boss who barks decisions into three phones at once while crisply giving orders to hovering subordinates. This is more fiction than fact. True, you often will have to make quick decisions without as much information as you would like to have about the problem. But on major decisions you usually can and should take plenty of time to select the best possible decision.

Your main obstacle to making good decisions may be fear. Few people actually enjoy making decisions. Many managers are, in fact, disturbed by a recurring anxiety: What if the decision is a bad one? What if it explodes in my face? With this fear dominating their thoughts, they may feel it is better to make no decision at all rather than to take the chance of making a wrong one.

As a potential supervisor, you may worry about this problem. Be reassured by the fact that no one makes correct decisions all the time. In matters that require human judgment, there is seldom a decision without some disadvantages. Whichever course you choose, there is usually something to be said in favor of its alternative. No doubt you will make mistakes, particularly at the beginning of your managerial career. What counts, however, is your overall performance as a decision maker. If you have a reasonably respectable batting average, you should be willing to face the prospect that you are going to strike out with a few of your decisions.

Is the ability to make good decisions inborn? To a degree, perhaps. But good decision making also calls for a methodical approach to solving problems, and this can be learned. It is this methodical approach that you can learn and practice as part of your self-development program.

10. Creativeness

As a supervisor, you will frequently face the need to

come up with creative solutions to tough problems. Two of your key subordinates may be unexpectedly absent, yet you must meet an urgent deadline. How do you do it without them? One of your subordinates, formerly a top performer, has slumped badly. How can you bring him back up to his former level of productivity? You have to reduce the cost of manufacturing a part in your department. How can you do it without reducing the quality as well?

As with decision making, many potential supervisors are uneasy about their ability to be creative when faced with such problems. The notion prevails that the ability to have ideas is exclusively reserved for born geniuses like Einstein and Edison. And yet it was Edison himself who said that genius was 10 percent inspiration and 90 percent perspiration. This is exaggerated, of course, but it makes a valid point: that there is far more to creativeness than simply waiting for a light bulb to flash over your head. You cannot increase your innate creativity—but you can learn how to use it to the fullest. The chances are, if we go by the evidence of psychological research, that you are not now realizing your potential for originating ideas and solving problems.

It is for this reason that we are including creativeness as one of the skills that you can improve in your self-development program. New ideas and solutions to problems are created by changing old ideas or experiences, by processing or manipulating them. We combine them in new ways, put them in a new context of time or place, add other ideas, take something away, change their color, meaning, purpose. To make the most of your creative ability, you can learn how to loosen up your mind so it will be receptive to new ideas and how to use a methodical, organized ap-

29

proach to solving almost any problem you are confronted with.

11. Initiative

No matter what your job, initiative is a useful quality to have—even if only to help you progress to a better job. But in a supervisory job, initiative is an absolutely essential ingredient in your managerial mix. A supervisor must *make* things happen, he cannot just let them happen. He must move on problems quickly before they grow to insurmountable proportions. When he sees opportunities for improving his department's performance, he must seize them immediately and not wait for someone else to push him into action. In other words, a supervisor must have the capacity and the willingness to act on his own responsibility without being prompted, urged, or directed.

Ironically, a man who has used plenty of initiative in his rank-and-file job often demonstrates less of this quality when he is promoted to managerial ranks. Because he has more at stake now, he plays it safe, fearing that by rocking the boat he will jeopardize his new status. In some cases, this may be a realistic reaction to the attitude of his superiors. But most enlightened executives these days are pleased to see their first-level supervisors displaying initiative, because they realize that it helps the organization. As one chief executive of a large metals company put it: "You don't get superior performance from people who are afraid the boat will rock; you get it from the ones who want to help row the boat."

This is not to say that as a supervisor you should go off

in all directions, acting independently of company policy and of the rest of the organization. A wise supervisor tempers his initiative with judgment. Good sense will tell him when he should move on his own and when he should consult higher management. During your early months as a new supervisor, you would be wise to spend some time identifying areas in which there is no question about your right to take action without first securing specific direction or permission from your superior. There are many areas of this kind where you could feel free to exercise your initiative with the knowledge that you would not overstep your authority or leave yourself open to criticism if you were not completely successful.

There are specific, down-to-earth ways in which you can develop this vital asset to your supervisory performance. Later on, we suggest some of the exercises you can do during your self-development program that will help you increase your initiative.

12. Flexibility

A manager, it is said, should be tough-minded but flexible. To many supervisors just starting out in their managerial careers, this may seem like a confusing contradiction in terms. Their mistake lies in thinking of tough-mindedness as stubbornness and flexibility as vacillation. This probably would be true if one element were present in your makeup without the other. But when both are present, each tempers the other so they become assets, rather than liabilities, to effective supervisory performance.

When a supervisor believes he is doing the right thing,

31

he must, of course, hold firm to his convictions. Otherwise he will simply bend whichever way the breezes blow. On the other hand, he must also be open-minded enough to listen to dissenting opinion and change his mind if the argument is persuasive enough. Pursuing a stubborn course for fear of losing face gets supervisors into trouble.

There are many kinds of flexibility a supervisor must have on his job. He must be willing to modify his goals or revise his procedures in the light of changing circumstances. He must adapt his approach to motivating an employee to the particular needs of that employee, rather than use a standard approach for every employee in his department. He must be ready to switch his plans in order to capitalize on an opportunity that comes along unexpectedly. He must be willing to negotiate with other managers for what he wants, rather than insist on complete and immediate victory.

Finally and most importantly he must be receptive to change. The supervisor who learns one way of doing things and stubbornly sticks to it despite the need for innovation will not survive long, because the world will simply leave him behind. Change is a way of life for today's supervisor, and he must adapt to it or perish. New organization forms are being developed, new methods are replacing old, new management technology is being devised, new products are constantly created, the computer is invading every aspect of an organization's work, new kinds of employees are on the payroll—indeed, the very goals of business organizations may be undergoing modification.

All this affects the supervisor because he often must not only accept change himself, he must persuade his subordinates to accept it. It is an unending role—as soon as you have completed the job of selling and implementing the introduction of a new machine, a new method, or a new man, you face the challenge of yet another change.

Moreover, your role is not only to accept change but to create it. You must be constantly developing new and better ways to do things in your department, even if they mean discarding methods and approaches that have been used for many years. You and your subordinates may be more comfortable with the old ways, but you must learn to leave the security of tried-and-true methods and explore the benefits of new ones.

In a sense, flexibility takes more courage and self-confidence than does inflexibility. Psychologists say that the flexible mind has a tolerance for ambiguity. It realizes that things are not black and white but often gray and that to see merits in only one approach, one method, one course of action, or one kind of person is to have a closed mind that cannot function productively in a managerial role.

Recognizing inflexibility in yourself is more difficult, of course, than recognizing it in other people. If you analyze your attitudes objectively, however, you may find that you are not as flexible as you might have thought. This is not an insurmountable problem. Your flexibility can be increased through conscious effort and through some exercises we suggest for your self-development program.

How Important Are These 12 Skills and Abilities?

These then are the basic supervisory skills and abilities, the tools you will use in successful management. All of them are necessary in practically every supervisory position, but they will vary in relative importance from job to job. A supervisory job in a steel mill, for example, would require a different mix of skills than a supervisory job in a bank, while a supervisory job in a hospital might require still a third mix.

This means that one of the essential preliminaries to designing a development program that will meet your needs is to learn the relative importance of the 12 skills and abilities in your organization. Your best source for this information should be your own supervisor. You might ask him to put in writing how he rates the 12 skills according to the following scale:

> Most importance: 3
> Average importance: 2
> Least importance: 1

If practical, ask supervisors of other departments to make the same ratings. There may be some differences in the results, but you should find a fairly consistent pattern in their ratings.

Supplement their judgment with your own, based on your observation of your supervisor at work and your analysis of your department's functions, methods, and personnel. Try to be objective; don't make the mistake of rating a particular supervisory activity as being important only because you like doing it or because you do it well. Letting such factors creep into your ratings will distort them badly, and this, in turn, will lead to distortion of your self-development program.

When you think you have achieved a valid consensus on the relative importance of the 12 skills and abilities,

Figure 2. How important are these 12 supervisory skills and abilities in your organization?

Skill or Ability	1 Least Importance	2 Average Importance	3 Most Importance	Comments
1. Functional ability				
2. Planning				
3. Organizing				
4. Controlling				
5. Oral communication				
6. Written communication				
7. Company orientation				
8. Leadership				
9. Decision making				
10. Creativeness				
11. Initiative				
12. Flexibility				

you may use Figure 2 to enter your results. Later on in the book, you will rate your present degree of competence in each of these skills and abilities. Then, by combining the importance ratings with your competence ratings, you can arrive at an overall development rating that will pinpoint the areas on which you should concentrate in planning your self-development program.

New Trends and Challenges You Will Face

$\mathbf{A}$ MAJOR and growing part of a supervisor's job today is the management of change—and this trend will accelerate during the 1970s. As we pointed out in Chapter 2, the supervisor must not only accept change himself, but he must take an active role in making it work and he must help his subordinates to cope with it.

What are these changes? How will they affect the supervisor's job? What can he do about them? The answers are not easy, because change, by its very nature, is not precisely predictable. Yet we know that certain major trends are already having or will have a profound influence on the supervisor's job. The more that you, as a potential supervisor, know about these trends, the better prepared you will be to meet the challenge they create. This chapter describes briefly the most important of these trends.

Let us start with changing technology. There was a time in American industry when an employee would learn his job and then do it in exactly the same way for the rest of his working life. Now it is a far different story. Jobs are constantly changing as a result of our exploding technology, and many completely new jobs are being created. As new equipment and new methods are developed, employees must be retrained to utilize them.

Their supervisors, of course, must keep up with these technological changes as well. This is not easy, because today a supervisor's subordinates may represent more than one kind of technology. But regardless of the effort involved, a potential supervisor must keep technically up to date in his field and continue to do so after he enters the managerial ranks. He may have been finely trained for his present position, but these days even excellent training can become obsolete after only a few years.

Along with the increasing technological complexity of today's jobs has come another trend: the emergence of professionalism. Employees who share the same expertise tend to identify with each other rather than with the company that employs them. Thus technicians and engineers view themselves primarily as members of those professions first, and then as employees of XYZ Company.

The implication for supervisors is clear. They must find ways to motivate these employees that fit in with their new concept of themselves. Only by acknowledging and accepting this professional attitude on the part of his subordinates can a supervisor motivate them to do their best.

The Computer

The computer, although relatively new, dominates the technological landscape like a Mt. Everest. It is no longer arguable that computers are changing almost every aspect of our lives. And as a supervisor you will certainly feel the impact of that change. You can react to it in one of two ways: (1) by making the most of the new opportunities the computer offers or (2) by digging in your heels and hanging onto the status quo. It may well be one of the most important decisions you will make in your career.

What do we mean by "the computer"? Actually, we are not talking about automated hardware. As a supervisor, you may never even see the computer that your company owns or leases. We are talking about electronic data processing (EDP): printout, spinout, runoff, or whatever name your company's EDP men give to computer-generated reports. What we are concerned with is the computer's ability to spew out facts and figures fast, and how that ability can be used by supervisors to do their job better.

Even if your company does not own or lease a computer, it is probably buying outside data processing services. Today, there is hardly an area where the computer is not reaching out to affect the way work is done—production, quality control, safety, traffic, warehousing, distribution, personnel, public relations, advertising, research, marketing, sales, purchasing, ordering.

For example, personnel supervisors of a business machines manufacturer are using computers not only for obvious statistical work, such as payrolls or absenteeism and tardiness analyses, but they are also using them for matching job applicants' qualifications against job requirements.

A monthly analysis of personnel performance tells the field sales manager of a sewing machine company which of his salesmen are paying their way and which are not.

The quality control manager of a razor blade company gets reports breaking down blade manufacture by grinder, by steel vendor, by shift, by inspector, by defects, by furnace and retort, and by position in the retort, with costs and comparisons to standards.

Why have computer appplications grown so quickly? What are the advantages of using computers? Here are five basic advantages that are particularly important to supervisors:

1. *Computers produce hard facts.* The supervisor who can act on facts is relieved of the anxiety of acting on educated guesswork.

2. *Computers work fast.* One dollar's worth of a computer's time can buy ten years of a manual calculator's multiplications or several hundred years of pencil and paper work. The speed and frequency with which the supervisor receives reports from the computer means that he can take immediate action on problems and also take preventive action when problems seem likely to arise.

3. *Computers do the drudgery.* Because computers store facts in infallible memory banks, do all the arithmetic, and print many different analyses from the same basic information, there is much less paper work, detail work, and tedious record keeping for the supervisor. This frees him for other important parts of his job that require human judgment, such as motivating, communicating, delegating, and training.

4. *Computers promote planning.* EDP gives supervisors more time and more facts to plan with. The facts

show a supervisor exactly where he is and where he is going, making it considerably easier to get where he wants.

5. *Computers improve cost control.* Because costs and
standards are broken down into fine details—dollars and
cents, hours and minutes, parts and people—the supervisor
has tighter control over his operation.

The computer's immense capabilities have led to the
creation in many companies of what is formally called a
management information system (MIS). Such a system
treats the company as one vast information-flow unit, dis-
regarding traditional department alignments or methods
of gathering and reporting data. The emphasis is away from
the conventional kind of accounting controls and toward a
dynamic system that continually assesses live information.
Thus data from all parts of the business are collected at the
data processing center where they are analyzed and interpreted at high speeds. Modified instructions are then sent
back to operating centers.

Decision making will depend more and more on sophisticated mathematical techniques that have been impracti-
cal until now because computers were not available to
process all the data quickly. Actions in each department
will be meshed with quotas and plans of other departments, and all will be geared to achieve the objectives
plotted for the company as a whole.

For the supervisor, integration of all company operations will mean that everything in his department must
click as never before. Slipups and deviations that were
formerly absorbed within one department's slack can now
affect the whole company. Accordingly, the supervisor
must be more alert than ever, exercising constant vigilance
over every detail, and reporting every fact that can influ-

ence the overall picture. He must see himself as an essential part of the feedback system, making sure that staff departments get complete and prompt information on completions of or deviations from schedules, as well as other changes that can affect the work in other departments. The supervisor must always keep in mind that a simple change introduced into his segment of the total process can necessitate compensatory changes in other areas.

As the computer increases its role, the supervisor will have other responsibilities too. He must sell his subordinates on the new ways of doing things. He must be the go-between who translates the new, mathematical decision-making concepts into meaningful terms for his subordinates. He must cooperate closely with staff specialists and other supervisors. He must be alert for ways to apply a computer program to the jobs in his own department. Data already available in his department could possibly be fed into the computer to give him more accurate predictive controls. (The computer can make various comparisons, decide whether one amount is equal to, less than, or greater than another, and carry out the necessary arithmetical operations *only* if it is fed a program, predetermined and put on cards or tape, to direct it to a next logical step based on the outcome of the preceding step.)

What can you do to prepare yourself for being a supervisor in the computer age? First, you should be willing to learn more about EDP, how it works and how it will relate to your managerial role. This does not mean that you must become a mathematician or engineer or that you must be able to operate a computer or write a computer program. But you should attain some knowledge of the new techniques to help you recognize what the computer can and cannot do as well as enable you to better analyze the information you receive from the computer.

Operations Research

Today, business decisions are so complex and have such far-reaching consequences that conventional decision-making procedures can too often lead to costly mistakes in judgment. Fortunately, new analytic tools and the techniques that go with them are being developed to improve the efficiency of business decision making. The foremost is called operations research (OR). Although as a first-level supervisor you will not be directly involved in using this technique, it will affect you and your job. As it becomes more widely used, and as you continue your climb up the managerial ladder, it will become more and more important to you.

Operations research is used primarily for major business decisions, such as determining what products a company should develop for five years from now or how much money it should spend on its advertising budget. Basically, OR is a method of data analysis utilizing complex mathematical techniques made possible by the computer's speed in calculating. OR men begin by defining, as precisely as possible, the nature of the problem as well as the ultimate objective. They recognize that certain actions will probably cause certain results, and they try to take into consideration all factors that might influence the structure of the situation. They then determine the probability of certain occurrences under all possible variations of these conditions.

Let us translate that into a simplified example. Suppose your company's advertising department wants to know whether to raise its ad budget, lower it, or keep it as is. The advertising manager might use several techniques to find the answer: He might examine company records to see how over the past few years advertising expenditures influenced sales. He might compare his advertising budget with those of competitors. He might make a field survey to gather fresh data. He might assemble all this and other information, forecast the level of sales for the period in question, and make an educated guess as to the amount he should spend on advertising. In short, he would arrive at a recommendation based primarily on *experience.*

On the other hand, an OR analyst might begin by formulating the problem in mathematical terms, like this: "Let P equal the probability that X number of consumers will buy our product during Y weeks; let L equal our level of advertising expenditure; let E equal the proportion of ad expenditures directly affecting sales of our product . . ." and so on.

Following this step—determining the various factors in the problem—the OR analyst would then assume certain relationships among them and create a mathematical equation reflecting these relationships.

The OR analyst does not actually recommend a course of action. He says, in effect, that if the company does so-and-so, here is the statistical probability of its return and risk. He plots all possible courses of action and their probable results and presents them to management for its decision.

The decisions you will face as a first-level supervisor are not complex enough to justify the operations research technique. But as a part of your efforts to broaden your perspective, you should be familiar enough with operations research to be aware of the role it plays in the major decisions that affect your department.

PERT, MOST, and CPM

In recent years, various planning control techniques for coordinating complex projects have been developed by systems experts. Originally designed as an aid in planning large defense projects, such as the development of a major weapons system, these techniques have also been adopted by many nondefense companies to improve the accuracy and quality of their own planning. A supervisor can easily utilize them in simplified form to work out schedules for his own departmental projects. The three most widely used of these techniques are PERT (program evaluation and review technique), MOST (management operation system technique), CPM (critical path method).

Although the three techniques differ in their details, they have a number of things in common. First, they are *network diagram* methods for the planning, scheduling, and control of nonrepetitive projects. Second, all three techniques provide means of showing in graphic form the answers to a set of questions posed before a program or a project begins:

How long will each job take?

What job or jobs must be completed first?

What job or jobs can be done at the same time?

What job or jobs cannot be started until other jobs are completed?

To give you an idea of how these new planning techniques work, Figure 3 provides a simplified example of CPM. A few minutes of study should be enough to show you how as a supervisor—or perhaps even in your present job—you could use this method to coordinate the activities involved in a project so that each activity will be completed in time to prevent the delay of other activities that are dependent on it.

New Approaches to Organization

The neat organization chart hanging on a manager's wall used to change very little over the years. Now, in many organizations, this chart is changing constantly, but if it isn't, it may not mean much any more in real terms. The growing complexity of management in all kinds of organizations, whether they be business, government, health, education, or other, demands more flexible organizational patterns than the rigid vertical hierarchy traditional in the past.

One reason for this development is that work in organizations is becoming less and less routine in nature. Take industrial production, for example. Companies used to turn out one product, or a few products, that were unchanged over the years. Because production itself was static, the organization could be static. No longer is this true. Now most companies not only make frequent changes in their existing products, they are constantly developing completely new ones. As a result, continuous production has changed into a series of separate projects requiring the skills of people from many different functional areas in the company.

Figure 3. The critical path method in action.

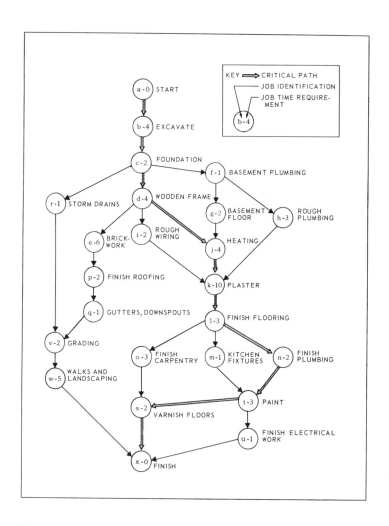

The simplified arrow diagram of a house-building project on the facing page shows how the critical path method works. In each circle, the letter identifies the job, and the number indicates how many days it is estimated the job will take. No job can be started until the job connected to it by the preceding arrow has been completed.

There are 22 different possible paths from Start to Finish, with total times ranging from a minimum of 14 days (path a-b-c-r-v-w-x) to a maximum of 34 days (path a-b-c-d-j-k-l-n-t-s-x). The latter path—indicated by dotted lines on the diagram—is the critical path. It determines the overall project time and tells which jobs are critical in their effect on this time. If the contractor wants to complete the house in less than 34 days, it would be useless to shorten jobs not on the critical path. It may seem to him, for example, that the brickwork (e) delays progress, since work on a whole series of jobs (p-q-v-w) must wait until it is completed. But it would be wasted effort to rush the completion of the brickwork, since it is not on the critical path and so is irrelevant in determining the total project time.

Instead, the contractor should examine the critical path for possible improvements. Perhaps he could assign more carpenters to building the wooden frame (d), reducing that job from four to two days. Note, however, that this would reduce *total project* time by one day, not two. The reason: Although the wooden frame will now take only two days to build, the next job, installing heating equipment (j), cannot start until the basement plumbing (f) and the basement floor (g) have been completed, and these jobs will take three days. Therefore, since (d) is no longer a critical item, the critical path could change, now passing through jobs (f) and (g) instead of (d), and only one day would be gained. Now that (f) and (g) are critical items, the contractor should examine the possibilities of completing those jobs in less time.

Our exploding technology is, of course, an important factor behind changing organizational patterns. As technology accelerates and becomes more sophisticated, each department within an organization becomes increasingly dependent on the activities of every other department. This means the manager must deal with other managers over whom he has no authority but through whom he must get work done. His lateral relationships are becoming as important as his relationships with his subordinates and his boss. Not only that, he must also consult technical specialists whose "authority" is not their position on the organization chart but their expertise, on which the manager must depend for correct decisions.

The trend, then, has been away from people working permanently in a functional department and dealing only with others in that department toward a system in which people from different departments form a temporary group and work together on a specific project.

One example of this new kind of organizational structure is known as *matrix management*. Matrix management deliberately violates what has long been a golden rule of management: *One man shalt have but one boss*. In a matrix organization, an employee may report directly to one boss as part of a line organization, while reporting functionally to one or more managers of other departments. For example, in the airframe industry, a propulsion engineer would report to the manager responsible for propulsion—but he also might be reporting to the managers of several design groups working on separate projects.

The supervisor in a matrix organization will find himself facing some unique problems because he must share control over his subordinates with other managers. When

48

two managers want the services of the same employee, it is a situation that calls for delicate negotiation. To make a successful transition to this kind of organizational setup, the supervisor must first broaden his outlook so that he does not think only of his own department but of what is best for the company as a whole. Departmental parochialism is a sure way to make a matrix organization fail.

To be successful in a matrix organization, a supervisor must be able to work cooperatively with people who are outside his department and over whom he has no authority. His skills in communication, negotiation, and persuasion will be put to the supreme test when he is dealing with a manager to whom he is not formally tied by company structure.

As a supervisor in a matrix organization, you will also have the responsibility for helping your subordinates adjust to the new patterns. Matrix organizations make special demands on the cooperative ability of every employee. It is up to the supervisor to teach his subordinates how to function with two or more bosses.

Difficult as it may seem, the matrix organization is proving to be extremely successful for complex manufacturing processes. Indeed, this new kind of structure may become increasingly prevalent, and the time may arrive when the standard organization will have disappeared. To have any success as a supervisor, you must learn to work effectively in this new kind of organizational environment.

Our Changing Workforce

That the nation's workforce is changing has been obvious in recent years. The directions in which it has been

49

changing—and will continue to change—are not quite so clear-cut. It is of paramount importance that any potential supervisor know as much as possible about the changing workforce because these are the people he will be called upon to direct and motivate. The more aware he is of the problems and opportunities presented by new kinds of workers and new employee attitudes, the better he can prepare himself to manage his subordinates effectively.

Interestingly enough, our workforce is developing in divergent directions. At one end of the spectrum, employees coming into the workforce are better educated and better trained than ever before. At the other end, there are increasing numbers of disadvantaged members of our society who are not only poorly educated and trained, but are often not oriented toward concepts of life and work that are commonly accepted by middle-class employees. At the same time, the younger workers in both of these groups will have values markedly different from those of their elders. And, finally, many of the women employees coming into the workforce will be demanding more equality in the world of work, thus upsetting some cherished stereotypes long held by the American male.

Ultimately these trends should have a positive effect on American business and industry and our society as a whole. But, as with any period of change, there are bound to be serious problems. The supervisor, because he is most directly involved with the new workforce, must deal with these problems. Let us discuss some of them.

More highly skilled employees. Innovation in products, processes, and procedures is bringing more and more highly skilled personnel into business and industry. This means that the supervisor of today will have to do some innovating of his own in his ideas about supervision if he is to make the most effective use of these talents. Concepts that have worked successfully with relatively unskilled employees may not be right for handling trained and educated people. Here are some of the requirements the supervisor of today's highly skilled personnel must meet:

1. More skill in supervision will be demanded to meet the needs of creative and professional people.

2. Supervisors will need ways of stimulating creativity in highly talented people.

3. Flexibility should be the key factor in a manager's approach to the well-educated employee.

4. Managers themselves will need broader, more thorough training.

5. Long-range planning and the "big view" will be increasingly important.

If you yourself are a trained professional or technical specialist, you will find it relatively easy to make the transition to supervising subordinates who have a similarly high degree of training. If not, you should prepare thoroughly to meet the problems of leading, organizing, and controlling a department in which you may have a number of such employees. There will be such problems as communication, for example. Each specialized field seems to develop its own jargon that can short-circuit communications in a department and, in fact, throughout the whole organization. Although this specialized vocabulary serves an essential purpose in communication among specialists of a particular field, it can impede communications with those who lack their training.

Also the supervisor must adjust his supervisory approach to the highly trained employee. The more skilled an employee is, the less a supervisor should be involved with direct supervision of him. His role should accent facilitating and coordinating rather than overseeing.

Attitudes of younger workers. We are living through a period of transition in which many long-established and seemingly inviolable ideas are changing. In the forefront of espousing new values are naturally the members of the nation's younger generation. And many of them are coming into the workforce.

Depending on your own point of view, this fact may or may not alarm you. Regardless of your attitude toward changing values, however, it is incumbent upon you as a supervisor to deal as fairly and open-mindedly with the younger generation as you would with any employees in your department.

Younger workers may tend to strongly question accepted beliefs and accepted ways of doing things in a business organization. In a sense, this is good, because it forces the supervisor to come up with persuasive justification for the methods and goals he is espousing. If he finds he cannot do so in every case, he may even modify some of his own attitudes, and he should not be afraid or ashamed to do so.

The supervisor's major problem with the younger workers—as with all of his subordinates—is to find the best ways to motivate them toward realizing their full potential as productive employees. To do this, he must look upon younger workers as individuals who have their particular needs and desires. What we are saying is that although younger workers *are* different from older workers in their values, their style of living, and their way of communicating, they are not a strange and alien race. Indeed, should the supervisor appear to regard them as such he will surely —in their own language—turn them off and lose them as potentially superior employees.

As social attitudes evolve and change and as new patterns of behavior emerge, the supervisor must continually search for appropriately relevant methods and concepts to help his subordinates become fully productive.

Employing the hard-core unemployed. More and more companies are concerning themselves with one of our most pressing national problems: the hard-core unemployed. As business and industry, in cooperation with government, are finding ways to successfully hire and train the "unemployables," supervisors will be increasingly faced with the challenge of managing them.

Who are the hard-core unemployed? According to a government definition, to be classified as hard-core unemployed a person must be poor and unemployed and fall into one or more of the following five categories: (1) under 22, (2) over 45, (3) handicapped, (4) school dropout, or (5) member of a minority group.

Many of these people will enter industry with substandard education and poor or nonexistent past employment records. Most of them have never had the chance to develop accepted work attitudes and have never been exposed to an industrial environment. Some may even have police records. Others may be people alienated from society through earlier dependency on institutionalized relief, welfare, and health services. Many have developed a feeling of powerlessness and a "don't worry about tomorrow" attitude. They may have a negative self-image.

Because a member of the hard-core has probably never worked steadily before, he has not developed the basic habits of attendance and punctuality. He has never had to be at a specific place at a specific time before, and the mere fact that he has a job will not imbue him with this concept. Because he and his supervisor will normally come from completely different backgrounds, he will probably be extremely suspicious of everything his supervisor says and does.

All this demands patience, understanding, and special approaches on the part of the supervisor who wants to turn his disadvantaged subordinates into productive workers. Attempts to motivate them should be aimed at building their trust and confidence. Training must be modified to fit the employee's special needs. The reasons for departmental and company rules must be explained to the hard-core employee even more thoroughly than to the more typical employee.

Women employees and equal opportunity. If you are a woman, you probably don't have to read this section. You are undoubtedly aware—perhaps painfully—that there has been serious discrimination against women employees in our society. Male readers, of course, may not be so ready to concede this. But whether they do or not, male supervisors must face the fact that their women subordinates—particularly the younger ones—may display more aggressiveness than before in demanding equal treatment.

Not too long ago, discrimination against women created nothing but laughter among many men. However, two major factors have forced male managers to take the subject more seriously. One, as we have already mentioned, is the new attitude of many women themselves. Another is the Civil Rights Act of 1965, which specifically forbids discrimination against women employees. Thus increased utilization of women's job capabilities is being hastened by law.

As more and more women become permanent (not just until marriage) wage earners, it is inevitable that they should begin to compete with men for the better positions. Women now comprise more than one-third of the U.S. workforce; in the 1940s the figure was one-fourth. Many companies are awakening to the possibility that women can do jobs that were always thought suitable for men only. And this includes being supervisors, both in factory and office, a fact which some male supervisors may view as a threat to their security. If such supervisors looked at this trend more objectively, they would probably accept it as simply part of the competition that normally exists for all managerial jobs. The crucial question about a candidate for a promotion or for a job should always be: Is he or she the best person available for the job? And it should be answered on the basis of that individual's qualifications, not on any stereotyped ideas about men or women.

The movement to provide equal job opportunities for women is not a fad that will soon pass away. The change in attitude is a substantial one that is rooted in the principle that every person should have opportunity equal to his ability. The principle is simple and just, but applying it is not easy. It is another one of the major challenges that today's supervisor will face in this era of fast-moving change.

The Dizzying Pace of Change

We have discussed only a sampling of the many trends with which a potential supervisor should be familiar. Actually, change is occurring in almost every area of our lives at a faster and faster rate. It would be impossible, and it is not really necessary, for you to know exact facts and figures on each and every one of these changes. That's why we don't expect you to know all the answers to the quiz questions on change that appear in Figure 4. Its purpose is not to test your knowledge but to convey the almost unbelievable magnitude and pace of change in our society today. If you are startled by the answers, we will have achieved our purpose, and you will have developed a new awareness of how rapidly things are moving.

Figure 4. How well-informed are you about our fast-changing society?

1. There are _____ blue-collar workers than white-collar workers in the U.S. today.

   _____ more
   _____ fewer

2. _____ percent of all the scientists who ever lived are now alive.

   _____ 50
   _____ 75
   _____ 90

3. In 1968, more than _____ new products were introduced into the consumer packaged-goods market.

   _____ 6,000
   _____ 9,500
   _____ 11,700

4. Of these new products _____ percent survived for at least a year.

   _____ 40

   _____ 20

   _____ 10

5. The average 20-year old employee today can be expected to change jobs at least _____ times during his career.

   _____ 2

   _____ 4

   _____ 7

6. There are now more than _____ computer installations in the United States.

   _____ 32,000

   _____ 35,500

   _____ 39,500

7. Since the beginning of this century, more than _____ percent has been slashed from the average time needed for a major scientific discovery to be translated into a useful technological form.

   _____ 30

   _____ 45

   _____ 60

8. Between March, 1967, and March, 1968, _____ Americans changed their place of residence.

   _____ 18,400,000

   _____ 26,250,000

   _____ 36,600,000

9. Organizations engaging primarily in one-of-a-kind projects rather than routine work will employ _____ percent of the total U.S. workforce within 30 years.

   _____ 30

   _____ 65

   _____ 95

10. At the rate knowledge is growing today, by the time a child born today graduates from college the amount of knowledge in the world will be _____ times as great as now.

    _____ 2

    _____ 3

    _____ 4

11. Within a recent three-year period, _____ of the 100 largest industrial companies in the U.S. reported major organizational shake-ups.

    _____ 32

    _____ 45

    _____ 66

ANSWERS

1. Fewer	4. 20	7. 60	10. 4
2. 90	5. 7	8. 36,600,000	11. 66
3. 9,500	6. 35,500	9. 65	

Your First Steps
on the Road to Promotion

YOUR decision to try for a supervisory position will trigger a whole series of moves on your part, adjustments you must make, and situations that you must deal with in your new role as a supervisory candidate. One of the first things you must do is call management's attention to the fact that you *are* a supervisory candidate. Like a political candidate, you will probably not be elected unless you toss your hat in the ring.

You may expect to be considered for a supervisory job without making any overt bid for it. If you view yourself as the logical candidate for a supervisory position that is vacant, it is pleasant to assume that you will automatically be given consideration. This is probably an unrealistic assumption in most cases. You would be lessening your chances of promotion by failing to let management know of your serious ambitions and your abilities that you feel justify that ambition.

Although you will eventually have to attract the attention of management several levels above your own supervisor, it is your supervisor who will play the most important role in furthering your career. He knows you the best —or he should—and it is his initial nomination that will put your foot on the ladder. One point should be made clear: We do not mean he should know you socially outside the workplace. That can be helpful, but what counts is the knowledge of you that he obtains from your daily contacts on the production floor or in the office.

Once you have made your decision, you should tell him that you are a candidate for promotion—both to let him know and to get the benefit of whatever advice he may have to give you. Just telling him is not enough, however. Your actions must support your words. For example, your basic job performance should be superior in terms of output, quality, and costs. Never fear that doing a first-rate job in your present position makes you so indispensable that promotion will be withheld. Nor does it hurt to occasionally volunteer for a tough or unpleasant assignment. You don't have to take them all—just enough to let your boss know that you are willing to pitch in for the department when you can help.

There are other ways to gain management's attention and at the same time develop your managerial potential. If your company, for example, has a voluntary presupervisory training program, by all means join it. In addition to being introduced to many new and fascinating concepts, you will have a chance to evaluate your competition. In most cases, management will make it quite clear that you should infer no promises of promotion from taking the program. However, these classes can certainly boost your chances. Many of the techniques and ideas you learn can be used on your present job, thus giving you an opportunity to show your talents to an observant management.

Another sure-fire way to gain favor is by contributing constructive suggestions to help the organization. Look around for improvement possibilities that may not be the responsibility of any specific person in your department. By coming up with creative suggestions, you will establish yourself as someone with initiative—a highly prized attribute of any manager. Your own supervisor will be grateful for ideas that will improve his department, since this reflects well on him in the eyes of his superiors. A useful safety suggestion is a possibility, as is a cost reduction idea. The ideas don't have to be momentous: any helpful suggestion will demonstrate to management that you are dedicated to furthering the interests of your whole group and of the company.

On the other hand, don't be afraid to think big in looking for ways to improve company operations. Just make sure that the change you suggest will pay off within a reasonable amount of time. For example, say you have an idea which requires a capital investment by the company. You might ask the controller what the company's time limit is for the amortization of its capital investments. Seek out the counsel of company engineers if you think they can help you with technical information. Of course, your suggestions do not have to be limited to technical matters. If you have ideas on improving employee relations or other areas, don't hesitate to volunteer them. Such ideas will attract the favorable attention from management that you are seeking.

Besides initiative, another attribute you'll want to demonstrate is company loyalty. Here again, action speaks louder than words. A good time to show your loyalty is during this period when, though you are still not a supervisor, your intentions to be one are clear. You have already begun your disengagement from your work group. No matter how long it is before you are actually promoted, your fellow workers will realize that you have made an irrevocable decision to become a manager, and that you are no longer a member of their group. This is the best time for you to demonstrate your commitment to management. If you give a good account of yourself at this point, the question of company loyalty will probably never arise again.

How do you demonstrate company loyalty? You do it every time you show that you have the organization's interests at heart. You do it with every suggestion you make for reducing costs or improving efficiency. You do it every time you volunteer to help a fellow employee with a work problem. These actions will not escape the eagle eyes of higher management. And such actions not only demonstrate loyalty, but show that you have the broader perspective that a supervisor needs. You are concerned not only about your own performance, but about that of the entire crew and the whole company. Your job is to make management aware that you have these attitudes so necessary for successful supervision.

Another way to show your broader perspective is to

increase your community volunteer work. Most company management believes that a good supervisor should also be a good citizen of his community. You can demonstrate your good citizenship by getting even more deeply involved in your community's activities than you may already be—so long as you do not overdo it to the detriment of your job performance.

During this whole period, you should maintain especially close contact with your supervisor, since he is the key to your eventual promotion. Remember, that your boss has a stake in this game as well as you. He knows that if he picks the best supervisory candidates he'll look good in the eyes of *his* boss. Therefore, he will protect himself by nominating only those people he believes will do him credit if they are promoted. The responsibility is on you to call attention to your qualifications, but without being obnoxious or boastful.

Communicate with your supervisor freely and openly. Seek out his counseling, not just to flatter him but because his advice should be worth your time and attention. He has experience with many situations and problems that you have not faced yet. Your respect for him is a critical element of the supervisor-subordinate relationship. You don't have to like your boss—but you should give him the respect he deserves. He, in turn, will probably be delighted that you are inviting him to help you with your development. By seeking his counsel, you are getting him involved in your progress and increasing his commitment to your success.

There are many ways in which you can call yourself to your supervisor's attention and build up a solid, rewarding relationship with him. For example, you might ask him to give you a more detailed appraisal of your job performance than he ordinarily does. You know that to be considered for promotion you must do an outstanding job. Therefore, you need to know where you stand in your work group. If your supervisor compares your work, detail by detail, with the work of other members of your group, you'll have a good idea of how you stack up against your competition. You can't feel competitive against an industrial engineering standard, but you can against a fellow employee who is also trying to improve.

By increasing your contacts with your supervisor you will be gaining his attention, and you will be absorbing the supervisory outlook by easing into the new perspective you must acquire to be a successful supervisor yourself.

To get the most value from your contacts with your supervisor, we suggest that you keep a record of them. Such a record will help you keep track of your development progress.

As a result of your decision to try for supervisor and your initial efforts to call yourself to management's attention, several things will happen. First, your boss will let *his* boss know that you are bidding for promotion. As a result, you will have more contact with your boss's boss than you have had up to this point. Perhaps your boss will take you with him to a staff meeting to discuss some facet of the department's work with which you are particularly involved. Perhaps he will ask you to take on a special project beyond the usual scope of your job—a project that will bring you into contact with other members of management at various levels.

Once the ball starts rolling, supervisors you have never met before may go out of their way to become acquainted with you. Perhaps they will take you on a tour of their area and go into some detail about their operation. Nothing overt will probably be said about your ambition to be a supervisor, but you will be getting some good orientation from first-line management in various departments.

Middle managers may seek you out, too. Their reasons for contacting you will be vague, but you will be aware of a rather intense scrutiny on their part. These meetings may even be social gatherings away from the work scene.

How do you handle these new situations? It will be natural for you to feel tension and excitement, of course, but your best bet is to remain—outwardly, at least—as calm and relaxed as you can, while still being alert. You are undergoing the classic management screening process which always precedes any decision on whether a supervisory candidate will make the grade. It may be a tough process to go through, but you should be glad it is happening to you. After all, managers are a select group. Much of your organization's success, in fact, will depend on how select it is. Management is not interested in choosing just a first-line supervisor. They want to promote men and women with the potential to rise through several levels during their career. From your standpoint, this is all to the good. If you are ambitious, you certainly won't be satisfied to remain a first-line supervisor forever.

Observe two cautions: Do not seem to be seeking special contacts with managers, but do not seem to be bowled over when they occur. One of the most important factors that managers will judge you by is how you react in a pressure situation. They want to see if you keep your cool under pressure rather than become outwardly upset or anxious. As you know from your own experience, it is not too

65

reassuring to have your supervisor come unglued in a crisis.

Along with scrutiny by management, you may have another ordeal to face when you become an obvious candidate for supervision. Your fellow workers will inevitably react to your change in status, and some of their reactions may not be easy for you to take. Those employees who feel that you are being disloyal may refer to you as the "company man," the "headquarters spy," or other terms less printable. If they are particularly bitter, they may even try to sabotage your promotion efforts by not cooperating with you on the job. Many fellow workers will not resent your ambition, of course, but even they will probably feel that their formerly free and easy relationship with you will have to change.

It creates a difficult situation that will severely test your determination to become a supervisor. During this period you are still technically a member of the working group while not fully belonging to it—and you are still not in the supervisory group. Being in limbo like this is not pleasant, but like the management screening process, you can handle it if you stay cool. Concentrate on doing your job. Make sure your performance doesn't suffer despite the difficulties. Consider the situation a test of your ability to handle unpleasant problems. You may get sympathy from your supervisor, but do not expect anything more. He, too, is watching to see how you cope with the kind of stress you will have to live with once you are a supervisor yourself.

In spite of these trying problems, don't think that this period will be nothing but unpleasantness. If you have the stuff of which supervisors are made, you will enjoy the challenge and excitement involved in this time of transition. Above all, try to maintain your perspective and sense of balance. Remember that dealing successfully with the challenges you face during these critical months will give you the confidence you need to master equally difficult situations that you will undoubtedly face during your managerial career.

5

Getting in Shape
for Your Development Program

A FEW years ago, William Blackie, then president of the Caterpillar Tractor Company, was asked what qualities he sought in the company's managers. Part of his answer was:

"We want people who are willing to work at their own self-development, not those who would sit back with an attitude which says, 'If you want me to be a better man, develop me.' To develop their capacity, we will give employees reasonable help, but we will not spoon-feed them. We don't believe in depriving people of the opportunity to be the architects of their own future."

This, of course, states one company's policy. Others might put more emphasis on formal training programs for their potential supervisors. (We speak of such programs later.) But no matter what degree of formalized training an organization gives its supervisory candidates, the chances are that its management would agree with Blackie's statement. The supervisory aspirant who lacks enough drive to undertake his own self-development program probably lacks enough drive to be a successful supervisor at all.

Drive, however, is only one of the requirements for a successful self-development program. Many ambitious employees have the drive to start such a program, but eventually drop it in discouragement. Their reasons: They cannot find the additional time that the program takes, they cannot get all the necessary reading in, they are in a perpetual state of exhaustion, and they just do not seem to be making any progress.

All these problems can probably be traced back to lack of adequate planning and preparation for their self-development program. This kind of project is not something you can embark on casually and expect success. It does take time and it does tax your physical and mental resources. But there are some effective ways in which you can minimize these difficulties, and we discuss them in this chapter.

Squeezing Out the Extra Time

Lack of time is probably the reason most commonly given for letting a self-development program peter out. You are working hard at your job, every moment of your day is filled, you have off-the-job obligations as well, and you certainly cannot completely neglect your family or your outside activities. Despite this, what you think of as lack of time may actually be caused by your misuse of the time you have. In his book, *Parkinson's Law,* C. Northcote Parkinson tells us that work expands to fill the time available. To a certain extent, the opposite is true also. Work can be made to contract and to liberate time not thought to be available.

The first step in finding out if you could be using your available time more productively is to conduct a survey of exactly where your day goes now. This exercise will pinpoint areas where you can squeeze out the extra hours you need for your self-development program, and it can actually be *part* of your program, because efficient use of time is one of the most important assets of a supervisor.

To learn how you spend your precious minutes every day, try logging your daily activities on a time sheet like the sample one in Figure 5. You should include time spent off the job as well as on, since much of your self-development program must be pursued during your off-job hours. Changes from one activity to another are indicated by an "x" on the time scale. Additional columns show what was actually accomplished, and what improvements could be made to save time. It will take practice to determine manageable activity units. For example, "Pick up a pencil" is too minute to be measured economically, while "Spent the day replacing defective wiring" would be too large because this might cover other activities such as coffee breaks, lunch break, and perhaps a department safety lecture by your supervisor.

The question of how detailed the record should be and how many days constitute an appropriate time unit must be answered by each individual. If you feel that a week is enough for a representative sample of the way you spend your time, use a week. If you work and live in a situation

Figure 5. Time log.

Date: 4/6/– –

Time	Activity	What accomplished	Timesaving ideas
9:00	Coffee and conversation.	Nothing.	Get started earlier.
	Went through in-basket.	Looked at papers and put them back.	Act on in-basket items immediately rather than go back to them.
	Filled out spec forms for vendors.	Did only six forms in an hour— too slow.	Suggest that forms be simplified—many items on it are never used.
10:00	Phoned Jack about poor quality of ABC Company's shipment.	Three minutes discussing shipment and fifteen minutes discussing Jack's fishing trip.	Keep phone calls more businesslike.
11:00	Daily meeting with Phil in receiving department.	Discussed next day's schedule and examined damaged shipments.	Schedule this meeting in the afternoon. This will save traveling time because I'll go directly from daily meeting with Bob to receiving next door.

where there are wide variations in activities within a month, consider recording for a month.

When you have completed your log, analyze it carefully. Examine each activity you have listed, and ask yourself how you can reduce the amount of time you are taking

71

to accomplish it. Here are some of the possibilities you might consider:

Look for short-cuts. Because you have always done a task a certain way does not mean it is being done the best way. There are often ways to revise and streamline routine chores. You might, for example, investigate and adopt timesaving techniques that other employees use on similar tasks.

Try to work on one task and complete it. You may notice from your log that you habitually do things piecemeal. For example, you may start checking some correspondence, then you suddenly remember you have to make a phone call to another department, then you see a note on your calendar to order a new typewriter pad, and so on. Each time you go to something else, it means you have to shift your mental gears, and this wastes time. Interruptions may sometimes make it impossible to finish a task, but your own self-discipline can save much time.

Keep your supplies adequate and well-organized. If you work at a desk, you may be surprised to find out how much time you waste looking for stamps or running to the supply cabinet for paper clips. If you are a production employee, just as much time can be thrown away by running out of parts or maintenance supplies. Maintain an adequate supply of things you need daily, and have them well organized so that you can find them when you want them.

Get started fast. The first half-hour of the work day is often completely wasted with unproductive activities like sharpening pencils, window gazing, coffee drinking, and chatting. If you are guilty of this habit, it adds up to two and a half wasted hours a week that you could devote to your self-development program.

Utilize your nonproductive time. Look over your log—aren't there many times when you are doing something necessary but nonproductive, such as waiting in line at a supermarket or riding a bus to and from work? Since these tasks require no mental attention, you can often utilize them for your self-development program. For example, you could read or you could do some planning of future activities in your program.

Avoid the telephone trap. If you use the telephone in your work, resist the temptation to indulge in friendly but unproductive conversation. Decide in advance what you want to accomplish during a call, know area codes and extension numbers, have all necessary papers and information in front of you, and keep your calls businesslike. You will save many valuable minutes.

Know when you work best. All of us seem to be more alert and energetic at certain times of the day. Analyze the ups and downs of your own energy during the day, and plan your most difficult tasks for the times when you are at your peak—that way you will get them done faster.

Vary your schedule if you need quiet time. To provide yourself with time when you can concentrate without interruption, try coming to work early before other employees arrive. Or vary your lunch hour, by eating early or late, so you can have a quiet period in your workplace.

How to Improve Your Reading Efficiency

Much of your self-development program will consist of reading books, magazines, and other text material. If you are already a proficient reader, your adjustment will be relatively easy. But many of us do not read as fast and efficiently as we are able to. If you are a slow reader, even the time you save from the suggestions we have just offered will not be enough for you to get in all the reading that you should. That means you must attack the problem directly by increasing your reading speed.

How fast should you read? Every individual's reading speed capability varies, of course. But it is safe to say that if your normal reading speed is 275 words per minute or below, you will find it impossible to accomplish the reading required for a successful supervisory self-development program. Preferably, your reading speed should be at least 600 words per minute—and you should aim for 800.

Be reassured that a gain in reading speed does not mean a loss in comprehension. Actually, it works just the other way. Your comprehension will improve, too, if your faster reading is done correctly. This is because speed reading involves reading complete phrases rather than individual words. This technique reduces the number of times that you stop and focus your eyes to a new position as you move across the printed line. It does more than save time; it improves comprehension by eliminating excessive pauses. Phrase reading also encourages the reader to abandon some common bad habits—namely, vocalization, subvocalization, and unnecessary physical movement of lips and facial muscles. Although subvocalization involves no perceptible lip movement, it is an actual sounding out of words in one's mind, a phenomenon known as "inner hearing." Both vocalization and subvocalization act as brakes on effective reading simply because the mind interprets words many times faster than we can say them. Getting rid of these habits can speed up reading considerably.

The principle of phrase reading is quite simple. Several words are read at once, rather than one word at a time. The object is to focus your eyes on word groups or "thought units." You might try this for yourself in reading the rest of this chapter. Try to absorb each phrase at a glance; avoid focusing your eyes on individual words. Mentally reflect, as you go, on each phrase's meaning.

Although you can probably improve your reading speed just by practice, you can do even better with expert guidance. Formal training programs are offered by schools in many cities. Or the do-it-yourself market offers a number of guides on improving reading skills, so that you can teach yourself speed reading. You will also find books on the subject in your library or bookstore.

Improving your reading efficiency is not just a matter of reading faster. Here are some easy-to-follow suggestions that will make your reading more productive.

Create a good reading environment. For someone as busy as you probably are, this is not always easy because, as we have suggested, you may have to cram your reading into odd moments when you have no control over conditions. But when you can, make sure that you have good light for reading, preferably from a double source to wash out glare. This will help to prevent eye fatigue and strain, which can be distracting. When you read, don't sink lazily into a soft chair or lounge on a sofa. Try for a compromise between relaxation and tension. You will often be doing difficult reading that requires alertness, and too comfortable a chair or sofa will put you to sleep. As much as you can, try to make the time and place of your reading habitual. You will then begin to associate this location and time with concentrated reading habits. If you do your reading at home, let your family know that you do not want to be interrupted by anything except a dire emergency such as the house catching on fire.

Clear your mind. You cannot possibly get rid of *all* the problems that plague you, but you can seal off some of them in order to read with fuller concentration. For example, if there is a telphone call you have to make, get it over with before you start your reading, so that it won't be nagging at the back of your mind.

Determine how thoroughly you should read the material. Not everything you read should necessarily be read in detail, so you should always skim the material first. Do this by studying titles or main headings, reading the preface and table of contents of books, or the opening paragraphs of reports and articles. If some section of the material strikes you as particularly important, read the opening and closing sentences of the paragraphs as well. Then look at any illustrations or diagrams. Once you have done this, you should be able to spot the main ideas of the material and decide on its importance to you. At this point you should also be able to tell whether the material is easy or difficult to read.

The evaluation you put on each piece of reading matter will determine how you read it. Some material will warrant no more than your initial skimming because the content is either already familiar to you or is not helpful to your study purposes. With other material, you may want to go back and pick out all the main points. Look for the topic sentence in each paragraph, which often but not always is the first sentence. It gives the central thought of the paragraph. Once you have found it, skip to the next paragraph. In other cases, you may want to fix the major details in your mind as well. Again, look for the topic sentence in each paragraph and pick out the details most closely related to it.

Material that you consider of top importance should get intensive reading. This kind of reading calls for maximum concentration and should be done when you are least tired and least likely to be interrupted. This is particularly true when you want to retain the details of what you are reading. If this is necessary, follow these four steps:

1. Concentrate on the need to remember. This will help you to retain the material more effectively.

2. Select key points as anchors for your memory. Authors often use headings, subheads, or numerical listings to outline their main points, as we are doing in this section. Look for these aids to fix the outline in your mind.

3. Whenever a logical break occurs in the material, restate to yourself, in your own words, the substance of what you have just read. In this way, you can summarize what you have read and reinforce your learning. If you wish to test your comprehension, refer back to the text.

4. Improve retention by repetition. By mentally reviewing newly acquired information from time to time, you will tend to remember it. If you have to assimilate a large amount of material, you should plan to spread the learning over several sessions in which you go over the same ground more than once.

Naturally, you cannot expect to remember all the important material you read. To get the most mileage out of your reading, you should establish a card file or reference notebook of what you read. When you come across an idea you can use or information that you may want to refer to, record it so that it will be retrievable when you need it.

There may be an item that has no direct use at the moment, but if your intuition tells you that it will come in handy someday, file it. It might provide the key to a major decision or be the basis for a new method or procedure.

Keeping Physically Fit

As we have mentioned, embarking on a self-development program on top of your already demanding job will put a strain on your mental and physical resources. If the stress becomes too great, you may either simply give up your program as being too much of a burden or you will slump in both your job performance and your self-development program. Although there is no ideal solution to this problem, there are ways in which you can make sure the strain is not too much for you.

Know your physical condition. If you haven't had a thorough medical checkup recently, now would be the perfect time to have one. Your doctor can tell you what precautions you should take to avoid overtaxing your health. He can also reassure you about any needless concerns you have about your physical condition. Surveys show that upon examination, most people usually have some symptom or ailment about which they are concerned. After examination, few of these people are found to have any significant trouble. Yet this needless concern can seriously affect your productivity and your mental state.

Live intelligently. It will be difficult for you to expend the necessary extra energy for your self-development program if your physical machinery is not in good operating condition. Intelligent living habits do much to insure the smooth functioning of your system. Proper nutrition, adequate rest, and regular exercise all contribute to vigorous health.

Of these factors, exercise is probably the most neglected. Our society is so highly mechanized and automated that most of us barely have to lift a finger to get our day's work done. And your self-development program will add more sedentary hours to your week.

Many people try to compensate for a sedentary work-week by going in for strenuous weekend sports. This is not the solution. By Monday morning, these people are exhausted and probably worse off than fellow workers who have spent the whole weekend in front of their television sets.

The key to healthful exercise is regularity. Fitness experts say that every adult should plan an hour of exercise each day as a basic minimum, to be supplemented by weekend sports and work around the house. The immediate reaction to this suggestion is usually, "Where can I possibly find an hour a day for exercise?" Actually it can be done with little loss of time, by working some simple exercises into your daily routine.

Perhaps the best all-around exercise is walking. It's easy and it has the advantage of convenience, since almost everybody can easily find time for a daily walk. You can walk to and from your office or plant or to and from the station, or you can take a walk at lunchtime or before going to bed. The walking you do on the job contributes, too. Ideally, you should walk at least 15 minutes three times a day, and make every step count. Breathe deeply. Don't walk so fast that you become short of breath; instead, walk just briskly enough so that after you're through, you feel as though you have really done something.

Watch your weight. Overeating in this country is a common problem. If you are overweight, you will find that losing pounds can mean gaining energy.

Get enough rest. One of the surest ways to drive yourself to exhaustion is to shortchange yourself on sleep. Even though your self-development program is adding extra hours to your schedule, don't steal those hours from the time you need for sleep.

Solve your problems. Being in a constant state of indecision can be mentally exhausting—and you won't have the extra stamina you need for your self-development program. Do something actively to stop the crisis between *yes* and *no.* That way you free your mind to concentrate on your self-development program.

6

Designing Your
Self-Development Program

WHAT you have read so far about the requirements and challenges of supervision may have left you somewhat discouraged. You may be telling yourself that you are not nearly ready to be a supervisor and that there is a bewildering variety of things you must learn. Our answer is simple: Of course you are not ready to be a supervisor. In fact, you will not really be ready even when you are promoted, because much of a supervisor's most important development occurs under actual battle conditions. And you do have many things to learn, but if you organize and pursue your self-development program in a methodical, logical way, you will perhaps be surprised at how quickly you begin to develop more confidence in your ability to make the grade.

Learning is hard work, but it is also rewarding work. You will receive the satisfaction not only of laying a solid foundation for your managerial career but also of being able to use your newly gained knowledge to function more efficiently in your present position.

Your first step in designing your self-development program is to set the goals you want to reach. But before you can take even that first step, you must go through an important preliminary: taking a personal inventory of your development position now. Only by pinpointing your specific development needs can you design a program that will prepare you most effectively for supervision.

You may feel that it would be impossible to evaluate your supervisory skills when you are not yet a supervisor. But if you consider the skills and abilities that we discussed in Chapter 2, you will see that you use all of them to some extent on your present job and some of them off the job as well. To refresh your memory, here is a list of those abilities and skills:

Functional ability.	Company orientation.
Planning.	Leadership.
Organizing.	Decision making.
Controlling.	Creativeness.
Oral communication.	Initiative.
Written communication.	Flexibility.

Looking over this list, you should be able to find some basis in your work or nonjob life for judging your competence on each of the 12 skills and abilities. To aid you in your self-evaluation, Figure 6 provides a checklist of questions. If you answer them as objectively as you can, they will guide you in estimating your qualifications as of now.

Text continued on p. 88.

82

Figure 6. Where do you stand now?

Functional Ability	*Yes*	*No*
Are you used to meeting obstacles to your goals—both on and off the job—and working through and around them?	___	___
Do you make a deliberate effort not to let personal prejudices and personality conflicts prevent you from functioning effectively on your job?	___	___
If you make a mistake, do you admit it and try to learn from it?	___	___
Do you face your problems squarely and act to resolve them rather than let them keep you in a perpetual state of anxiety?	___	___
Can you concentrate on your job even though you may be bothered by personal problems?	___	___
When an emergency arises, do you act calmly to solve it rather than panic or freeze?	___	___

Planning	*Yes*	*No*
Have you had much experience in planning long-range projects, either on or off the job?	___	___
Do you plan your work at least a week ahead so you know what you have to do and how you are going to do it?	___	___
Are you familiar with planning techniques such as PERT and MOST?	___	___
When you are assigned a special project, do you thoroughly plan your approach before you actually start working?	___	___
Do you consistently meet your deadlines?	___	___

Organizing	*Yes*	*No*
Have you had much experience—on or off the job—in assigning people to specific tasks in order to accomplish a larger goal?	___	___
Do you know how your department is organized in terms of different job functions,	___	___

83

how they are coordinated, who reports to
whom, who is responsible for what, and how
much span of control your supervisor has?

Does your job require much coordinating with
other employees in and out of your department?

Are you familiar with basic principles of organization and how organizational patterns
are changing in management today?

Do you have a fairly good picture of how your
whole company is organized?

Controlling	*Yes*	*No*

Does your present job involve spotting deviations from departmental schedules and
plans?

Do you know how the reporting system works
in your department?

Do you know how it works in your whole
organization?

Have you broken your job down into separate
elements and established standards for each?

Do you keep tabs on your performance by
periodically measuring it against your
standards?

Do you know how electronic data processing
works and what role it plays in your department's functioning?

Do you have a tickler system for reminding
you of tasks you must have done by a certain time?

Oral Communication	*Yes*	*No*

Do you spend much of your working time
talking and listening?

When you talk to people, do you find that
they usually get your message correctly?

Do you clarify your goals before you communicate on an important matter?

Could you tell a new employee how to do your job? — —

Do you get feedback so that you are sure your listener understands what you are saying? — —

When someone is talking to you, do you listen attentively and open-mindedly, concentrating carefully on what the speaker is saying? — —

Written Communication   *Yes*   *No*

Does your present job require that you write memos, reports, and letters? — —

Have you written any long (over 10 pages) reports on relatively complex subjects? — —

Do you do much writing off the job? — —

Do you approach a writing job with confidence in your ability to be grammatical, clear, well organized, persuasive, and readable? — —

If you are a technical specialist, do you think that you could write a report on your subject that could be understood by a nonspecialist in your organization? — —

Company Orientation   *Yes*   *No*

Do you know what your job contributes to the organization's overall goals? — —

Do you have at least a fair working knowledge of what function is performed by each of the other departments in your organization? — —

Do you know how other functions in the organization relate to that of your department? — —

Do you try to keep your boss informed on things that could affect the performance of your department? — —

Do you cooperate with staff people when they are implementing improvements in your job or department? — —

Do you pitch in willingly when there is extra work to be done? — —

Do you strive to keep costs down on your job, almost as if you were a stockholder in the organization? ___ ___

Leadership	*Yes*	*No*
Do other employees sometimes come to you for guidance on job problems?	___	___
When criticizing others, do you try to keep your remarks constructive?	___	___
Think of the employees in your department with whom you are most familiar. Could you describe the best way to motivate each one to do a better job?	___	___
Do you praise people when they accomplish something outstanding?	___	___
Do people tend to open up to you?	___	___
Are you willing to give someone else a task to do even though you know you can do it better?	___	___
Do you get along well with most of your fellow employees?	___	___

Decision Making	*Yes*	*No*
Are you accustomed to making important decisions in your job?	___	___
Have you developed a methodical approach to making decisions?	___	___
Do you face the prospect of having to make a difficult decision without dread?	___	___
Do you willingly accept the responsibility for your decisions?	___	___
Would you say that at least half of the difficult decisions you make turn out right?	___	___

Creativeness	*Yes*	*No*
Does your present job require that you use your creative talents?	___	___
When you hear about an innovation in another field, do you try to think of ways in	___	___

which it could be adapted to some aspect of
your own work?

Do you often think of better ways to do things, both on and off the job?	—	—
When you face a tough problem without any tried-and-true answer, can you usually come up with a creative solution?	—	—

Initiative

	Yes	No
In your present job, are you pretty much on your own in choosing your work methods?	—	—
Do you act on opportunities without being urged or directed?	—	—
If you have a problem on your job, do you try to solve it yourself before you go to your supervisor for help?	—	—
Do you usually participate vigorously at meetings?		
When you realize that something should be done, do you do it rather than procrastinate?	—	—

Flexibility

	Yes	No
When you run into opposition to your ideas or plans, are you willing to listen to the objections?	—	—
Are you alert to new trends that might affect you and your work?	—	—
Do you ever admit that you were wrong and change your mind about an idea, method, or person?	—	—
Do you try to see the merits in changes in departmental methods, and do you do your best to make them work?	—	—
Do you try to approach situations without preconceived notions, prejudices, and assumptions?	—	—
When on the receiving end of criticism, do you view it as an opportunity to learn and improve?	—	—

87

Rating

Skill or Ability	1 Strong	2 Average	3 Weak	Importance Rating	Development Rating
1. Functional ability					
2. Planning					
3. Organizing					
4. Controlling					
5. Oral communication					
6. Written communication					
7. Company orientation					
8. Leadership					
9. Decision making					
10. Creativeness					
11. Initiative					
12. Flexibility					

You may also want to ask yourself additional questions that may be relevant to your particular situation. Don't be afraid to admit that you are weak in a specific area. It will defeat the very purpose of your skills inventory to delude yourself about the areas in which you need the greatest development work.

After completing the checklist, calculate your overall development rating for each skill and ability by filling in the table on the last page of the figure. First, write down the appropriate competence rating—for example, if you consider yourself average in creativeness, write the number 2 in the "average" column. Then, refer to Figure 2 to find the importance rating on creativeness. If it is 3—most importance—write that number in the "importance rating" column. By adding your competence rating and your importance rating, you will get your development rating: 5.

Based on the possible combinations, your development ratings may run from 2 to 6. You can interpret these ratings according to the following key:

Rating 2: No development work needed.

Rating 3: Only maintenance work needed.

Rating 4: Least development work needed.

Rating 5: Average development work needed.

Rating 6: Most development work needed.

When you have arrived at your development ratings, you should consider discussing them with your supervisor. With his more objective view of your abilities, he may be able to point out areas where you have been too hard on yourself or areas where you are perhaps not as strong as you thought. His more detached evaluation will help you set sound, accurate goals for your self-development program.

You might, in addition, discuss your inventory with someone outside the company, such as a close friend whose opinion you value. Ask him for his candid assessment of your inventory. He can give you still another point of view that can help you to plan your development strategy more effectively.

Once you have established your development goals, your next step is planning how to achieve them. Here again, consultation with your supervisor and others can be extremely helpful. Your supervisor's most important contribution may be to suggest ways in which he can help you develop specific skills by giving you special assignments to make you stretch. For example, he could give you an assignment that requires more planning than you ordinarily do or delegate to you the handling of a periodic report in order to improve your controlling skills.

If your organization has a management development specialist, your supervisor may suggest that you consult him for further guidance in your self-development program. The management development specialist is usually a member of the personnel or industrial relations department. With his knowledge, he can give you expert direction in selecting the right activity to strengthen a weakness or further improve a strong point. He can advise you when to take a course, when to do intensive reading, when to design and carry out a special project, or when to consult a manager in another function of the organization.

Be sure not to bypass your supervisor when you are consulting the management development specialist and other people in your company. Let him know that you plan to see people outside the department, both as a courtesy and so that he can get a complete picture of what steps you are taking in your program.

For specialized knowledge about other functions in your company that you think you should learn more about, a manager involved in the specific function can help. As an expert in his field, he can suggest sources of knowledge to you or, if he is willing, he might even take the time to give you some training in the subject himself. Depending on your own functional area, you might ask for guidance from engineering, finance, quality control, maintenance, data processing, accounting, production control, systems, personnel, marketing, and so on.

Finally, the rest of this chapter can also help you to design your development program. It gives a rundown of the many different ways that you can improve your skills and knowledge. Necessarily, the discussion must be general, and you must locate the specific sources of training in your own organization and community. But the chapter can, we think, tell you enough about the different kinds of training and development activities to guide you in selecting the ones that are best for your needs.

In-Company Training

A training program for potential supervisors offered by your own company can have distinct advantages over training from outside sources. For one thing, because it is in the company, it will be tailored closely to the supervisory skills and abilities that are most important in your particular organization.

Another advantage of in-company programs is that they may be given on company time, so that your self-development will not be an exorbitant drain on your own time. Moreover, you will save traveling time, since most company training is given where you work. And the trainers in the program are easily accessible, so you can always consult them when you need individual help.

The training program in your company may have been designed from scratch by your own training department, or it may have been purchased from an outside management development organization. Even in the latter case the program has probably been adapted by your training department to the particular needs of the supervisory jobs in your organization.

Good as your company's training program might be, you would be wise not to consider it as all you need for your self-development program. It can be a basic foundation for your program, but it should probably be supplemented by training from other sources and your own study. For example, the company program may not give enough emphasis to a supervisory skill in which you need heavy development, such as oral communication. You should then seek other ways to develop that skill.

Noncompany Training Programs

If your company does not have a supervisory training program of its own, there may be outside programs available in or near your community. Such programs, although they will not be tailored to your company's particular conditions, can still be very helpful. They may be given by a government agency or by the adult-education division of a local college or local school system. You can probably get information on what programs are available from your personnel department or from a local chapter, if there is one, of the American Society for Training and Development. If there is a tuition fee for the program (some are free) ask your supervisor or personnel department if it is company policy to reimburse employees for job-related courses taken outside.

In addition to general supervisory training programs, you may also find individual courses that can be helpful. These may be offered by such organizations as city school systems, universities' extension centers, community colleges, or the YMCA. The courses offered by these organizations are far more varied than they were even a few years ago.

With individual courses, you can zero in on the intensive development of specific skills. For example, if you are particularly weak in written communication, you can probably find a writing course that will bring this skill up to an adequate level. You will find other courses, too, that will be useful even though they may not be directly job-related, such as courses in human relations, creativeness, and problem solving.

If you lack a college degree, and you have been told that this will hurt your chances of promotion, you might investigate the possibility of earning a degree at night. Most community colleges now make it possible to earn an associate degree at night, and many universities offer a baccalaureate degree through night courses.

Classroom training is an effective way of learning in a number of ways. First, it provides stimulating interaction with the instructor and with the other students. Second, you can measure your progress against that of others in the class. Third, you may be spurred by the competition among students that often arises in a classroom.

Correspondence Courses

For the employee whose company has no training program and whose community has no classroom courses available, correspondence courses can be an effective substitute. In addition, correspondence instruction has some unique features which may appeal to you:

1. You can progress at your own rate, which might be faster or slower than that of a class.

2. You can choose your own hours to do the homework. Even if you are on a shift operation, there is no interference with working hours.

3. No traveling is necessary.

4. Correspondence courses are generally cheaper than classroom instruction. This is important particularly if your company does not reimburse you for the costs.

Don't think, however, that learning by correspondence is easier than learning in a classroom, despite what some correspondence schools may promise in their advertisements. Any kind of learning is hard work. Moreover, correspondence courses don't provide the stimulation of a good classroom teacher or the give-and-take discussion of a class. Some people need this kind of atmosphere to maintain their interest. Furthermore, there are many subjects—like human relations and public speaking—in which discussion is an important part of the learning process. Finally, there is no way of earning a college degree through home study alone. However, most colleges and universities will permit one-quarter of the necessary degree credit to be earned from correspondence courses, and some will permit one-half. This credit must generally be earned through correspondence courses of accredited resident colleges and universities that have home-study departments.

Correspondence schools offer a broad variety of courses. For the would-be supervisor, there are such courses as manufacturing methods, mathematics, business correspondence, computers, office management, applied imagination, data processing, industrial sociology, and control-systems theory.

For a list of good correspondence schools, write to National Home Study Council, 1601–18th Street, N.W., Washington, D.C. When you receive the list, you can write to the schools most suitable to you for their course catalogs.

Programmed Instruction

Like correspondence courses (some of which utilize programmed instruction), programmed instruction is a form of individual study in which the learner proceeds at his own pace. Relatively new, programmed instruction is a unique method of organized self-instruction. Instead of conventional texts, where a chapter of material is followed by a set of questions, programmed material gives the student a small amount of information immediately followed by a question. These individual segments of knowledge are called "frames." Each frame in a course is composed of: (1) a simple statement, closely related to the statement preceding it, and a question to test the trainee's understanding of the statement; (2) provision for the learner's answer; and (3) a correct answer, which remains covered until the trainee is ready to check his own answer.

Each successive statement picks up and builds upon the

central thought of immediately preceding statements. This structuring not only gives the presentation continuity and coherence, but it also provides for the repetition of key ideas—repetition that assists and reinforces learning.

Programmed instruction is presented in two main forms: special teaching machines or textbooks. Available courses of study cover virtually all aspects of business and industry, from mathematics to human relations.

As a learning method, programmed instruction has advantages similar to those of correspondence courses: No teacher is required, course materials are self-administered, and each student can learn at his own pace. Courses of interest to the potential supervisor are available from such organizations as the American Management Association.

Books and Magazines

Reading books and magazines can be an invaluable supplement to the more formally structured sources of development we have discussed. Many books have been published on supervisory techniques, for example. You may find some of them in your company library. In addition to general books on supervision, you will find books on specific subjects relating to supervision, such as clear writing, human relations, accounting, electronic data processing, cost control, office management, leadership, group dynamics, and so on.

Periodicals can also be helpful. Some magazines, such as AMA's *Supervisory Management,* publish articles specifically aimed at helping supervisors be more effective in their jobs. Other magazines, such as *Business Week, Forbes,*

Management Methods, Dun's Review, and *Management Review,* are aimed at a broader spectrum of business readers, but can be helpful in giving you the wider perspective that you should have as a supervisor. Still other magazines, such as *Factory, Modern Manufacturing, The Office,* and *Modern Office Procedures,* are devoted to either industrial or office techniques. Finally, there are even more specialized publications, such as *Safety Maintenance, Chemical Engineering, Datamation,* and *Hospital Management,* that deal with specific fields or functions.

In most periodicals and in some books you will find only certain articles or chapters that will be worth your while to read. Here is where the preliminary skimming techniques that we discussed in the preceding chapter can save you time.

Programs Sponsored by Equipment Manufacturers

Equipment manufacturers are generally eager to present technical programs related to the proper operation and maintenance of their products. Since the programs are usually free, professionally prepared, and informational rather than promotional, they can be an excellent source for upgrading your technical knowledge of your particular field. Keep in mind that as a supervisor one of your major tasks may be to teach your subordinates how to operate and maintain complex equipment. These programs can help prepare you for this training job.

Of particular interest in this category is the four-day course given by IBM to provide nontechnical people with a basic knowledge and understanding of electronic data processing. Although it is not intended to make the learner a programmer, he goes through the steps a programmer takes, writes a simple program, runs it through the computer, and receives his printout.

Miscellaneous

If you are a professional, you can further your development by becoming active in the local chapter of your professional society. Familiarize yourself with the mechanics of your society, hold committee posts, and run for office. There is much to be learned from directing and motivating people who don't have to take orders from you, and there is much to be gained from hearing the technical information conveyed at meetings.

You might also attend the programs of local professional societies other than your own. Many accounting, training, purchasing, personnel, administrative management, and other professional societies invite prominent men and women to talk to their members about a wide range of subjects. Entrance fees are usually low; your company's representative may be happy to take you along as a paying guest.

If you lack self-confidence and effectiveness in speaking to groups, you might consider joining your local chapter of the Toastmasters Club. This organization gives a speechcraft course which will provide you with valuable experience making speeches and then listening to the criticism of your efforts by other participants.

7

Do-It-Yourself Projects
for Your Development Program

JUST as important as learning through training is learning through doing. In your self-development program, one approach should complement the other. What you are learning through your courses and your home study should be applied in actual projects that you can plan and execute yourself. In addition to reinforcing your learning, this will give you invaluable experience in utilizing supervisory skills and abilities. When you actually receive your promotion, you will have more self-confidence in facing many of the challenges of your new job because you will already have had some experience in dealing with them.

There are things you can do on your own to help in developing each of the supervisory skills and abilities we have been discussing. In this chapter we will suggest some of the possible projects you might undertake. Don't follow these suggestions slavishly. Adapt them to your own particular situation and needs. And by all means try to think of other do-it-yourself projects that might aid in your development.

Functional Ability

You probably have plenty of chances to exercise your functional ability on your present job. The problems and pressures you face may not be the same in kind or in degree as those you will face as a supervisor, but they do call for functional ability, and the skills you develop in dealing with them can easily be transferred to those you must deal with after you are promoted.

Off-the-job problems, too, can present useful opportunities for improving your functional ability. An unexpected domestic emergency, an unavoidable change in carefully laid vacation plans, or a driving accident can provide grist for your self-development program, because they force you to act under stress and pressure.

After each incident—either on or off the job—you should carefully analyze how well you functioned in the face of the problem. Were you able to accept the fact that something went wrong and then try to right it? Or were you completely thrown by whatever happened, so that you were not able to think calmly about what you should do next? How would you react differently the next time something like this came up?

If you think that your functional ability needs more severe tests than it gets normally, you might even seek out stressful situations, by joining a volunteer fire department or ambulance service in your community.

Planning

We don't know how much planning you do on your present job. Whatever the amount, however, it probably does not approach the complexity of the planning you will have to do as a supervisor, which means that additional practice in planning can be worthwhile.

First, ask yourself if more methodical planning could help you do your present job more efficiently. Even in a nonsupervisory job, it can often pay to plan ahead more than a day or even a few days. You will find it possible to utilize many of the planning techniques that you learn in your studying to set objectives and accomplish them more efficiently on your job.

In addition, you can undertake extra projects that require planning techniques. One of them, of course, is your self-development program itself. Then, you might set a long-range goal for improving your job performance—let us say, increasing your productivity by 10 percent within six weeks. To accomplish this goal will take planning skill.

Even off the job, you can apply the planning techniques you are learning from your courses and your reading. How about planning your summer vacation, for example? Or perhaps you are ready to add an extra bedroom to your house or build an outdoor patio. Projects like these give you a chance to practice your planning skills and at the same time make your project more successful.

Organizing

Unless you have responsibility for other jobs in your department, you won't have much chance to develop organizing skill in your regular job. However, you can certainly create such opportunities, both on and off the job.

On the job, there are often temporary projects being undertaken that require an employee committee. It might be a committee to study ways of improving safety procedures in the department or to devise ways of reducing departmental costs. Chairmanships of such committees often go begging because few people want to take on the extra burden they entail. This gives you an ideal opportunity to get in some practice in applying the organizing skills you are learning in your study program. When your supervisor starts an employee committee, be the first to volunteer to head it. You will then have the job of organizing the committee, deciding what each of its members will do, and coordinating their various functions. The experience will be invaluable to you.

You may have similar opportunities off the job as well. Think back—when you are asked to serve on a committee of a charitable, civic, church, political, or educational group, do you smile weakly and say you would love to but you are just too busy? If so, you are missing some excellent chances to practice your organizing skills. And even family projects, like the yearly bout of spring cleaning, can be used to develop these skills.

Controlling

You will also find that you can apply controlling techniques both on and off the job. On the job, you can use your growing knowledge of controlling to keep tabs on your performance in terms of production, quality, cost, waste, and so on. In addition, you might ask your supervisor to assign you to special projects that require the use of control techniques.

Off the job, you can apply control techniques to family projects such as those we have already mentioned or to any other outside projects in which you are involved.

Oral Communication

You won't have to look hard for opportunities to practice this vital supervisory skill since you probably spend a good deal of your time talking and listening both on and off your job. What may not be as easy as finding opportunities is making the most of them. Talking and listening come so naturally to us that it is often difficult to be self-analytical about how well we are communicating or to consciously apply the principles of better communication that we have learned. It will take a strong effort on your part, because using newly learned communication techniques requires mental alertness and concentration. But you will soon have the satisfaction of seeing that your oral communication is more effective and at the same time easier as you gradually begin to apply good communication techniques almost automatically.

Make a habit of doing a postmortem on every important piece of communication you do during the working day—whether it is with your supervisor, a fellow worker, or someone else. Do the same thing for the important oral communication you have off the job, too. Ask yourself if you were effective in your talking and listening, whether you accomplished the purpose of your communication, or whether you failed partially or completely. Examine each failure closely, to find out where you went wrong. If you feel it will help, keep a written record of each analysis, so that you can consult it when you are faced with a similar communication problem.

Written Communication

Whatever writing you do on your job provides you with a chance to practice the writing techniques you are learning through your study. If you don't have such opportunities on the job, create them. For one, ask your supervisor to keep you in mind for a special assignment that would involve the writing of a report. Or initiate a report yourself, perhaps to propose a change in departmental methods you think would improve efficiency. Writing such a proposal presents an ideal opportunity to work on developing such qualities as clarity, precision, organization, persuasiveness, and readability in your writing.

Off the job, too, you can find ways to practice your writing skills. You may belong to organizations that sometimes need volunteers to write reports, publicity releases, or announcements. The next time such an opportunity comes up, grab it. Similarly, don't overlook the chance to apply your newly learned writing techniques to your personal business letters.

Company Orientation

As we have said, company orientation is more of an attitude than a skill or ability. Nevertheless, like the other items on this list, you can develop and practice it both on and off the job.

One way to achieve a company-oriented attitude is to broaden your horizons. We all become absorbed in our own particular function in an organization, and this is only natural. But in concentrating on that small segment of the total operation for which we are responsible, we often lose sight of the bigger purpose of our job. Therefore, one of the best ways to develop a stronger company orientation is to learn more about what goes on outside your own limited sphere. This will help you to improve your conceptual skills—the ability to see a function or group as part of a larger concept rather than as an isolated unit. Conceptual skills will become more and more useful to you as you climb the management ladder and must oversee larger groups of both people and functions.

You might start out by examining your own work group more analytically. Try to see how the different jobs in your group mesh together to achieve certain objectives broader than that of any individual job. Then examine how your group interacts with others in the organization. You might keep a log of the contacts that people in your department have every day with people from other departments and what these contacts achieve as a contribution to company objectives. You will see that your department's interfaces with some departments are critically important, while others are relatively less important.

Try to learn as much as possible about your company's overall goals and its programs for achieving them. Then try to relate these goals and programs to what is happening in your own department. You will perhaps attain a clearer understanding of what is behind some of the changes in your department that were a mystery to you before.

From your research, you will develop a broader concept of your job in the organization. You can put this concept into practice in a number of ways. For example, you will be better motivated to contribute your ideas for improvement, both in your department and in the whole company. You can keep your superiors informed of the things they should know—both good and bad—about your department that will affect overall company performance. You can co-operate with employees from other departments and consider how your actions will affect their operations. You can speak knowledgeably of your company and its programs in your contacts with customers, suppliers, and people in the community. In short, although your job is important in itself, you will see it in a new light as part of a larger team striving for major long-range goals.

Leadership

Since in your present job you probably have no official authority over others, you may be dubious about the practicability of developing leadership skills now. Not so. Remember that, as we pointed out earlier, leadership does not consist of wielding official authority to get things done through other people. Thus practicing leadership without such authority is a good test of your leadership skills. If you want somebody else in your organization to do something, you can't *order* him to do it. Instead, you must utilize such skills as motivation, communication, and persuasion. And these are the very skills you will need even when you are officially in command.

One of the best forms of leadership practice is teaching. Such experience will be invaluable to you as a supervisor, because you will spend much of your time teaching others, either on a one-to-one basis or in groups. Inducting and training new employees, training to upgrade present employees, and introducing major changes in methods and procedures all involve teaching.

Beyond this, however, teaching is good practice for developing leadership because it involves such leadership skills as communicating clearly, motivating, morale building, problem solving, and developing subordinates.

You can look for teaching opportunities both on and off the job. If other employees in your department require a sharpening of their working techniques, you might suggest to your supervisor that you could spend some time helping them. You would then be able to practice teaching in an actual operating situation.

Don't overlook outside teaching possibilities, either. If there is a skill or activity in which you are an expert, how about teaching a class of Cub Scouts or a group of ghetto children? Besides contributing to your community, you will give a boost to your own leadership skills.

For more practice in leadership, you can volunteer to head committees in any local organizations of which you are a member. Here you will have authority tied together with responsibility—an important relationship for any potential supervisor to learn.

Decision Making

In the study part of your self-development program, you will learn the fundamental steps of good decision making, such as defining the problem, gathering the relevant data, exploring the alternatives, considering the probable consequences of each alternative, and, finally, selecting the best alternative and acting on it.

You don't have to be a supervisor to use these principles; you can start applying them right now to practically every decision you make on or off the job. You may feel that some of your decisions are too minor to warrant applying all the steps of methodical decision making—but do it anyway. The more you practice, regardless of the size of the decision, the more effectively you will apply your decision-making skill. So even when you are at the supermarket trying to decide between buying super colossal or merely colossal olives, practice your decision-making techniques.

You will find it helpful to record some of your more important decisions in detail. When the results of the decision are in, you can refer back to the thinking that went into it to see why the decision proved correct or incorrect.

Creativeness

The creative part of your mind must be given freedom and exercise to release its full potential. Fortunately, creativeness is something you can easily find opportunities to practice both on and off the job. And such practice is vitally important, because today's supervisor must be more of a creator, innovator, and experimenter than the supervisor of the past had to be.

In your studying, you will undoubtedly gain new insight into how the creative part of your mind works and how you can channel it into developing constructive ideas and solutions to tough problems. You can put that insight to work immediately, without waiting for promotion. One useful exercise would be to question the way you conduct every phase of your job. Isolate one aspect—for example, the way that you lay out the supplies you work with—and ask yourself some questions, such as, Why am I doing it this way? How much of it did I actually plan this way? How much just evolved haphazardly? How much is habit? How can it be done better?

You can also exercise your creative ability on a larger scale by looking for improvements in departmental methods and procedures. Every viable idea you come up with to improve department operations will accomplish three things: (1) It will help the company, (2) it will increase your promotion chances, and (3) it will strengthen your confidence in your ability to innovate.

Another effective exercise in creativity, and one you can do anywhere at any time, is to feed yourself a hypothetical problem of some sort. Ask yourself a question beginning with "What if . . .?" and then try to come up with creative solutions.

Finally, here is a simple exercise that has proved successful in a class in creative thinking. Take an everyday object and ask yourself how many different ways it could be used.

One class performed this exercise with an angle iron and came up with 128 different uses. When you perform this exercise, don't reject any of your ideas, no matter how wild they might seem on second thought. This is an exercise to free your imagination, not to restrict it.

Initiative

If you lack the initiative that is so essential to successful supervision, you can best strengthen this quality through practice. Your goal should be to undertake activities that are above and beyond your job description. By doing so, you will make yourself a likelier candidate for promotion. Just as important, with each successful exercise in using initiative that you perform, you will gain a little more confidence in striking out on your own without waiting for an order. On top of that, exercises in initiative can broaden your knowledge and experience and make your job considerably more interesting.

Your whole self-development program, of course, is an outstanding example of initiative in action. Many of the suggestions for specific exercises that we have made in this chapter involve initiative, such as thinking of improvements for your department's operations or studying the functional relationships between your department and others in the company.

One of the most important uses of initiative is to act upon a problem once you recognize that there is one. Usually, we tend to sidestep problems until we are forced to do something about them. The effective supervisor takes the initiative—he moves on a problem as soon as he is aware of it. As a result, he can usually solve it more effectively, because he is not under critical pressure at the early stage of the problem.

Look around for such budding problems in your own job or in the department as a whole. If it is something you can handle yourself go ahead and do it, and then let your supervisor know that you dealt with it. If it is something beyond your control, consult your supervisor so that he has a chance to move on it or perhaps to assign you to solve it.

Flexibility

Mental flexibility is often not easy to achieve, because our minds tend to become set in rigid patterns of thought that are difficult to dislodge. Yet flexibility is an essential quality in any supervisor who wants to deal successfully with the infinite and constantly changing variety of people, problems, and pressures he faces.

If, after objective self-analysis, you think you need more flexibility, you might undertake some of the following exercises:

• Try to listen with more of an open mind to what others say. Be patient, and try to understand their point of view before jumping to conclusions.

• Make a real effort to force changes in your habit patterns. For example, you might vary your reading habits. If you never read anything but mystery stories, why not try a historical novel or a nonfiction book on current affairs? How about a different kind of vacation from your usual one? Are you in a television rut? Perhaps you can break out of it by attending a play, a concert, or an art exhibit. We are not suggesting that you give up the activities you enjoy now—only that by doing different ones occasionally you will be breaking the mold of rigid habit and increasing your flexibility.

• Widen your circle of social contacts. Do you see the same people over and over again? Perhaps you should make a deliberate effort to meet people outside that habitual circle. One of the best ways to meet new faces is to serve on a voluntary board for a civic group, hospital, church, or charitable organization. Or you might try your hand in local political affairs. Any activity that takes you out of your immediate circle exposes you to new experiences and new opinions which can stimulate your thinking and increase your mental flexibility. You may find that the person sitting next to you does not think the way you do. You may have to articulate your own views to those who don't agree with you, and you may find that you learn much from other points of view also. The experience can be challenging and frustrating, but it is also excellent preparation for a potential supervisor.

Designing Your Long-range Plan

Once you have learned about the different types of training and study available to you and about the development activities you can do on your own, your next step should be to establish a detailed, long-range plan for your self-development program.

You may feel that such detailed planning is unnecessary, that you will simply pursue your development work every time you get a chance and let it go at that. It is true that since you are undertaking this program on your own initiative, you don't have to worry about meeting deadlines from your boss. But this simply means that you should be setting such deadlines yourself.

Why is this so important? Because if you don't establish specific goals—and deadlines for meeting them—you will end up floundering aimlessly and accomplishing little. You may spend too much time on one area of your development and not enough time on another. You will have no idea of what kind of progress you are making in any area. And you will not gain the feeling of accomplishment that comes from setting definite goals and then meeting them.

That is why we recommend that you use the form in Figure 7 to get your development plan down on paper. The overall time span you choose will depend, of course, on the particular goals you want to achieve. For example, if you want to earn a degree, your program might take two years or more. If your development ratings show a need for work on only a few skills, it might take as little as six months to accomplish what you have set out to do.

As you fill in the plan, try to be as specific as possible. For example, for "written communication" you might put down under "training and study," "Take writing course at Center City Community College, Thursday nights, 8–9:15, starting Feb. 2."

Under "do-it-yourself practice," you might put down, "Write four reports of at least ten pages each, two on technical subjects, two on nontechnical subjects." In the "completion date" column, you might put a date six months from now as your deadline for achieving this goal.

When you complete this form, you will have—in black and-white—the broad design of your self-development pro-

Figure 7. Long-range development.

Date: 2/5/– –

Skill or Ability	De- velop- ment Rating	Train- ing and Study	Com- pletion Date	Do-It- Yourself Practice	Com- pletion Date
1. Functional ability					
2. Planning					
3. Organizing					
4. Controlling					
5. Oral com- munication					
6. Written com- munication					
7. Company orientation					
8. Leadership					
9. Decision making					
10. Creativeness					
11. Initiative					
12. Flexibility					

gram. In the next chapter we show you how to use this basic plan to break your development work down into smaller time units so that you can keep tabs on your progress and achieve your long-range goals on schedule.

How to Achieve
Your Self-Development Goals

YOU will remember that in Chapter 5, on getting in shape for your self-development program, we suggested that you do a detailed study of how you spend your time on and off the job. Now you can see why this is such an important preliminary to planning your program. With this information, you can estimate with a fair degree of accuracy how much time you have available for your development work. Then you can work out a realistic schedule of your development activities.

By now you should have designed your basic development plan with its specific long-range goals and a timetable for meeting them. But in order to measure and maintain your progress toward these long-range goals, you must develop some short-range goals—or subgoals, if you will. You would do the same thing, for instance, if you were planning an automobile trip across the country. Let us assume that your long-range goal is to drive from New York to Los Angeles in seven days. If you simply start out and drive without looking at your odometer, a map, or signposts, you will have no idea of how much progress you have made after the first day of driving. You need short-range goals so that you can plan your drive. You might set a goal of 500 miles the first day, 450 the second, and so on.

Similarly, you need short-range goals for your self-development program. Your major problem will be to set them realistically. Your self-development program will contain a number of elements to which you must allot varying amounts of time. First, there is classroom training, on or off the job. Since the classes themselves have a specific time period, you will have no problem being precise here. Any homework you get, however, will be harder to measure in terms of time. You can get some guidance from your instructors if you ask them approximately how much time they think you should spend on homework.

You will also be reading and studying on your own. If you are taking a correspondence course, you will have no assigned deadlines; you may proceed at your own pace. You would be wise to set your own deadlines—for example, let us say one lesson a week. If, in your schedule, you have overestimated or underestimated the time it takes you to complete a lesson, you can revise your schedule to compensate.

Your own reading may also be hard to estimate in terms of time until you are able to gauge more accurately how long it takes you to go through a specific periodical or a certain number of pages in a book. Once you are more familiar with how much reading you can accomplish in a given amount of time, you can schedule your reading goals with a fair degree of precision.

Time required for do-it-yourself projects may be more difficult to pin down. Some of them may not require extra time because you will be doing them during your normal activities—such as practicing oral communication. Remember, however, to set aside time in your schedule for recording the results of such practice.

More formal projects that will require additional time should be worked into your schedule. If you undertake the writing of a report in order to improve your written communication skill, set a definite goal for yourself. It might be one week, two weeks, or a month, depending on how long you think the writing will take and how much time you can devote to it.

Try to be sensible about your time estimates for completing your short-range goals. Tasks usually take longer than we think they will. When you figure out how much time a specific project will require, add a little more time to provide a margin for unexpected slow-ups or problems.

To keep track of your progress, we would suggest using a week as the basic unit. Progress in practically any of your development activities can logically be measured in that span of time. Even if the total time of a specific project is longer than a week, you can measure your weekly progress on it. For example, if you are undertaking a planning project scheduled for completion in three weeks, you should have accomplished about a third of the work at the end of the first week, and so on. By keeping constant tabs on deviations from your original schedule, you can make necessary adjustments in the schedule early enough to be able to complete the whole project within the deadline. Or, in some cases, you may feel that the best alternative is to change the final deadline to a later date.

Try also to make your short-range goals specific rather than vague ones. Instead of writing down, "Practice oral communication techniques," say specifically, "Analyze at least three important oral communication contacts each week."

Don't attempt to cram development work on every skill and ability into each week's schedule. You would have to be superhuman to give a meaningful amount of time to every area in such a short span; therefore, your progress in any specific one would be infinitesimal. Aside from those skills and abilities that you will be practicing during your normal activities, it is advisable to rotate the various segments of your development program from subject to subject. Thus you can concentrate on two or three subjects for a few weeks, and then switch to other subjects. This will provide you with a period of intense work on each subject, while the change of pace every few weeks will keep you from becoming surfeited with any one subject. Keep in mind that you will need variety in your self-development program to maintain your enthusiasm.

Keeping tabs on how closely you stick to your plan will be an excellent exercise to develop your controlling skill. You can set up whatever system you think will serve your purposes, but we would suggest that you use a loose-leaf notebook and lay out a week's activities on each page. When you complete each week, check your progress against your long-range plan.

Be sure to consider your self-development plan as a flexible one rather than as something engraved in stone. Don't hesitate to revise it when necessary. You may find as you go along that one aspect of supervisory skill is taking more effort to develop than you originally thought it would. Or, on the other hand, you may easily master a skill in much less time than you had originally assigned to it.

Measuring your progress against the specific goals you have set for yourself is not the only way in which you should determine how well you're doing. You may be too close to the whole process to evaluate objectively your overall development. To get a better perspective, you might consult with your supervisor. He will be involved in much of your development work, and he should be glad to tell you what he thinks your progress is and how ready you are for promotion. He can be particularly helpful in evaluating you on projects which he himself has assigned, such as writing a report or training a green employee. Some of his comments may be critical, of course—and this can hurt. But keep in mind that you are consulting him for his objective evaluation, not for soothing flattery. It will do you far more good to be constructively criticized than to be deluded into thinking your progress is better than it actually is.

As you near the completion of your long-range goals in your self-development program, there are two possibilities. One is that you will be promoted to a supervisory position. The other is that you will not. This could happen even if your supervisor and other managers consider you ready for promotion. Keep in mind that there are always a limited number of promotions available—and more candidates than vacancies. In addition, the company's particular situation at the time you near the end of your self-development program may make your immediate promotion impossible. For example, a proposed major reorganization may have put a temporary freeze on all promotions in your division. Or a tight financial position may be slowing down promotions.

You should first consult your supervisor on this problem. If you are not satisfied with what he tells you, you can let him know that you would like to talk with *his* boss or the personnel department. It does no harm to let everybody concerned know that you are eager to be considered for the next available promotion to supervisor—as long as you are not obnoxious about it.

In consulting your supervisor and other managers, try to get as close an estimate as you can of how long it might be until a promotion. If it is a matter of months, your natural inclination might be to complete your self-development plan and then wait.

It would make more sense, however, for you to continue your self-development program—but with new goals that will stretch you even farther. You can reduce the intensity of your program to get some of your leisure time back, but keep at it. Like a boxer who must stay in training even when there is no immediate fight ahead, you should be keeping your skills razor sharp so you will be ready for the challenge when promotion day does arrive.

9

When You're Promoted—
Those First Critical Months

THE great day has arrived. You have won the promotion you worked so hard for—you are now a supervisor. Understandably, your warm glow of triumph is mixed with considerable apprehension. Despite all your preparation, you are still moving into the unknown and unfamiliar. You face a breaking-in period that will be full of challenge—but full of promise, too. The way you handle yourself in these first few months can give you a solid start toward success.

Move cautiously until you get a clear understanding of the people and procedures in your new department. Whatever you do, don't be impulsive or arrive at faulty conclusions on scanty evidence.

On the other hand, don't be too slow in establishing your authority. You do not have to use bull-in-the-china-shop methods to accomplish this. A wise manager seeks and accepts good advice, but vacillation or hesitancy during your first days can create a poor initial impression. Associates may assume that you lack decisiveness. You must make it plain to both subordinates and peers that you expect to run the department and will make key decisions affecting it. However, since you need their confidence and goodwill, you should show that you want their suggestions and recommendations. Never assert your authority simply because you are boss. A good leader delays action until he is reasonably sure of the proper move. But there is a difference between sitting still and studying a situation and simply sitting still because you are waiting for someone to tell you what to do.

If you have been promoted to supervisor of your old department, you may have trouble adjusting to your new relationships with your former co-workers. No matter how much you resolve that there will be no difference, this is really beyond your control. There *will* be changes. The very process of asserting your new leadership will in itself apply a great deal of stress to old friendships.

If you are supervising a department that is new to you, you will not have this readjustment problem, but you will have others. You don't know your new subordinates—their strong points and weaknesses, how much responsibility you can safely delegate to them, how to get the most out of their capabilities. You may have been given some advance information on their abilities and characteristics by your predecessor. This information can be useful, but don't allow it to prejudice your own personal judgments.

In analyzing your subordinates, remember that your presence as their new boss can have an unsettling impact on them. You represent change, and they are waiting to see how this change will affect them. Understandably, they are insecure and uncertain. The more firmly you take hold and reestablish their confidence, the more surely you can move forward.

Getting to know your subordinates does not mean you should butter them up or try to be one of the boys. It is important that you stay in character. The gregarious boss may do a splendid job, but it is not because he is a friendly and outgoing person. The real reason is that he knows his job. Subordinates realize that he expects their best at all times and that he doesn't hesitate to crack down when necessary.

On the other hand, there is nothing more futile than the naturally reserved, self-contained manager who tries to be something different because he thinks that is the way to win goodwill from his new subordinates. His attempts to step out of character will only make them uncomfortable.

Your relationships with other supervisors will also involve major adjustments. Some of your new colleagues will be old friends who were promoted before you. Others will be strangers to you. All of them will be eyeing you as the neophyte and making their private estimates of your chances for survival.

It may be difficult for you to make friends with your new peers on a personal basis, but those friendships you do make will tend to be meaningful throughout your business career. And your peer group, if properly approached, can be a gold mine of information and useful tips on good management.

You must be prepared, however, for possible clashes

with associates whose interests or ideas conflict with yours. If possible, defer any showdowns until you are well established and can defend your views with solid facts, rather than with generalities or emotional arguments. The more successful you are in avoiding personalities when you have business differences, the better you are able to perform your duties.

Always keep in mind that your new associates have been in their jobs longer than you have been in yours. Don't make the mistake of having a know-it-all attitude that will simply build up resentment against you.

You will also have adjustments to make in your relationships with your new boss. Paradoxically enough, your relationship may now become more formal than it was previously when you were a rank-and-file employee. Then, you may have been on an informal, first-name basis with many members of management within your own group. Now, this may be changed. Your new boss must avoid any appearance of favoritism or special privilege. Casual social contacts previously enjoyed will suddenly be curtailed if your boss is one who subscribes to the "no fraternization" school.

If the organization does maintain a highly professional posture among its management people, you may be baffled by the observance of protocol now demanded of you. You will be much more severely bound by the necessity of going through channels than you have been used to.

It is evident enough by this time that the transition period between being promoted to supervision and becoming an effective, well-integrated supervisor is crucial to your career. During this probationary period, you will be subjected to the closest scrutiny you will ever receive as a manager. Not only your immediate superior, but many echelons of management above him are keenly interested in your growth and development as a member of management. Your performance in the first few months on the job will govern whether you make it at all, whether you will be judged as a solid first-line supervisor but no more, or whether you are found to have the potential for several promotions during your career.

Your contribution to the success of the organization during this transition period will not be inconsiderable. You are at the interface between management and the worker, and it is your responsibility to get your share of the product down the line on time under the best possible conditions of quality and costs. No other member of the enterprise has a heavier responsibility than the first-line supervisor. It would be difficult to overemphasize the importance of establishing many channels of free and open communication at this time. The signals you send will provide upper managers with the data they need for their long-range decisions; those you receive will assist you greatly in the daily conduct of your job.

It would be remiss not to pause here and remind you, as a new supervisor, of the importance of your commitment and involvement in the overall success of the organization. Intellectual effort can never do the whole job; emotion has to enter the picture.

We can—and, of course, we shall—say "Good luck!" in your new career. But both of us know that from here on out it is your superior performance as a supervisor that will be responsible for most of your good luck.

Index